D1715897

Collected Poems

GEORGE WOODCOCK

Collected Poems

1983

Sono Nis Press

VICTORIA, BRITISH COLUMBIA

Canadian Cataloguing in Publication Data

Woodcock, George, 1912-
    Collected poems

Poems.
ISBN 0-919203-40-X

I. Title.
PS8545.O53A17 1983   C811'.54   C83-091114-6
PR9199.3.W58A17 1983

This book has been financially assisted by the Canada Council
Block Grant Program and the Government of
British Columbia through the British Columbia Cultural Fund
and British Columbia Lottery Revenues.

Published by
SONO NIS PRESS
1745 Blanshard Street
Victoria, British Columbia
V8W 2J8

Designed and printed in Canada by
MORRISS PRINTING COMPANY LTD.
Victoria, British Columbia

TO

Roy Fuller
&
Julian Symons,

POETS, CONTEMPORARIES AND FRIENDS

Contents

Mythology

Black Flag

A World at War

Eros and Thanatos

The End Man

Anima, or, Swann Grown Old

Translations

Collected Poems

Introduction

There are special considerations attending the assembling of a *Collected Poems* which are different from those applying to the preparation of an ordinary collection of poems. In the latter case the poet is — or should be — picking what he thinks to be the best poems he has written over a certain period, and however he may arrange his selected pieces, his criterion of choice will always in some way be excellence. But the *Collected Poems*, when prepared by the author himself, is in some way nearer to an autobiography than it is to an ordinary collection of verse, since now the poet is not concerned with showing his best work so much as with showing the work that adequately represents his creative career, and in the process he must reveal his weaknesses as well as his strengths. Indeed, he is not merely presenting a poetic autobiography in the selection and arrangement he makes; he is also preparing the ground for the serious criticism of his works, and this involves the awesome responsibility of offering everything he has written that seems to him worthy of eventual consideration.

This, of course, does not obviate selection; it makes it all the more necessary. There are many things a poet writes that even in the short run he does not consider worth submitting to journals, and even in the long run he may feel that he has perhaps written more poems of a certain kind than need be remembered except by research scholars. It is in the process of assembling a *Collected Poems* that these choices are implemented.

So in the poems and poetic fictions I here offer, I am not presenting everything I have written or everything I have published. At the same time, a very few poems that have never seen print do so here for the first time; they are mostly quite early pieces that did not achieve publication when I was young for reasons quite unrelated to their quality. But the great majority of the poems that follow were published, in British, American, Canadian and Australian periodicals too numerous to mention, and many of them have also been read in various radio programmes of the Canadian Broadcasting Corporation. One of them, "White," has been set to music in a choral arrangement by the Canadian composer, David Duke. Most have been included in one or other of the eight volumes of verse I have published, beginning with the *Six Poems* which Charles Lahr brought out in 1938 from the Blue Moon Bookshop in London, and continuing through *The White Island* (1940), *The Centre Cannot Hold* (1943), *Imagine the South* (1947), *Selected Poems* (1967), *Notes on Visitations: Poems, 1936-75,* (1975), *Anima, or, Swann Grown Old: A Cycle of Poems* (1977), *The Kestrel and Other Poems* (1978) and *The Mountain Road* (1980). A few poems have been written since the last collection appeared, and the translations that form the last section have never been included in a volume.

This collection includes all the poems I still think significant that I have written between 1933 and 1981. It does not include my earliest poems, nor even the first of my poems to be published, which appeared in the *New English Weekly* under A. R. Orage's editorship in 1932. While I had developed a considerable technical facility at that time, I did not really begin to speak in a personal voice until the poems of 1933, like "Sawmill" and "Winter Wheat," when I started to use imagist insights for my own purposes.

But though those first printed poems hardly have a place in the body of this collection, it may be of interest to reproduce one here, since it is fairly typical of the kind of verse young poets of the early 1930's tended to write before they found their own tones in their own time —the verse that came from reading Jack Squire's Georgian-oriented anthologies and A. J. A. Symons's collection of Nineties poets. The poem is called "Nocturne," and its strong visuality is perhaps what most links it to my later work:

> 'Tis even, day's dark requiem,
>   The grey gnats dance a rigadoon,
> And Venus, like a pendant gem,
>   Hangs from the girdle of the moon.
>
> A screaming heron homeward flaps,
>   Gaunt, like some demon drawn by Blake;
> A laggard swallow swoops, and laps
>   The pallid waters of the lake.
>
> Yon row of poplars blacklimned stands
>   Screening the sun's last hectic light,
> And lovers, with enclasped hands,
>   Worship the mystery of night.

I am not ashamed of "Nocturne." It is good pastiche and it might well be appropriately included among the juvenilia if a complete edition of my poems were ever made by a literary scholar. But a *Collected Poems* prepared by the poet himself is in some degree a moral as well as a literary act, and it can only present the poems by which, in his maturity, he is willing to stand, and by which he is willing to be represented.

In arranging the collection I have discarded as unsatisfactory the idea of a merely chronological sequence. One of my reasons is that my career as a lyrical poet has been broken by a great time rift. For reasons largely told in "Black Rose," I wrote very few poems between 1949 and the late 1960's, though I did write a number of verse plays. So instead of arranging the poems merely by their sequence in time, I have arranged them into eleven groups which, without necessarily having common themes, show clear affinities with each other. Within these affinity clusters I have followed a time sequence as far as possible, so that patterns of development can be traced. I have also, in the list of poems, appended a rough date for each of them. Where possible, it is approximately the year in which the poem was written; where that is not possible, it is the date of the periodical or volume in which it first appeared. On a few occasions I have been able to hazard no more than a guess, and I indicate such poems by a query beside the date.

I would express my gratitude to the editors, publishers and radio producers who in their various times and places thought so many of these poems worth publication, and to Robin Skelton who thought them worth assembling as a collection. Finally, in dedicating this volume to two old friends and fellow poets of the 1930's, Roy Fuller and Julian Symons, both born in the same year as myself, I am acknowledging ancient debts that cannot be forgotten.

G.W./1983

Southerndown Beach

Fluid ebon masses, flow
sculptured waves to broken snow
and, speedwell-eyed, delphinium blue,
sky to sea cleaves. Gleaming, new,
of cosmic conjugation born
clouds to the faint horizon spawn,
rise on the landward wind, impart
misgivings to the tripper's heart
and, hundred-browed, assault the sun.
Dancers' feet of ripples spin
up the firm sand. The swimmers glide
beachward on the swelling tide.

Summer Fire

Flowing across the shrivelled grass
the fire runs from the railway line
into the orchard, ringing the cherry trees
with hounds of fire.

Where the fire has passed
a carpet of sable;
brown and withered the cherry leaves.

Winter Wheat

The blue rosettes of winter wheat
form ranks in the yellow clay.
Their tarnished swords
are spread with sharp antagonism
in a barbed circle protecting their identity,
uncompromising selfness.
But they will grow,
washed by the rain of spring,
into tall slender brothers
leaning together,
whispering in gentle voices.

Sawmill

No tenor droning of the circular saw,
snort of donkey engine,
purr of belt over slotted wheels,
clatter of new planks stacked,
crunch of tires on the gravel,
no hoarse voices of men . . .

But black buildings stacked against the sky,
the dereliction of a rusting engine,
a tramp's fire winking behind abandoned cordwood . . .

Roses and Christmas Roses

I saw white roses on Christmas morning,
white buds of tight rose ivory,
never wide-blooming, never revealing their fulness
of intimate stamen gold
to cold grey winter skies.

And in the shadow of that same rose briar
white moon cups, stars
of clotted snow,
upborne
on shafts of green pale ice,
sun-avoiding,
in the shadow
coldly born and consummated.

A Farmer's Epitaph

Deep night upholds the heavy doom
Of roses over Sheppard's tomb,
And he who tore the acres lies
Where brain knows no Spring ecstasies.
In six by two of blue-green clay
Earth has her still revenge today.

Thames

The punts are laid up for a profitless summer;
Anadyomene, the virgins shimmer
Rising from the backwater, sunburnt and slimmer.

Fungoid in the meadows tents are built.
The trains are full and by the riparian halt
Their wheels crush out the detected master's guilt.

All weirs are dry, and foetid cords of slime
Drip from their steps to pools undashed by foam.
The anglers are playful, the virgins without shame.

And in the evenings the gramophones
Sing through the clotting dusk in metal tones
The amorous laments of stones and towns.

The anglers boast of escapades on cliffs.
Under the branches, from the swaying skiffs
Are heard the virgins' protests and the throaty laughs.

Ancestral Tablet

Night when mares escaping fought in the lane
Where apples went to fields in the glut year,
We talked in the sandstone kitchen as glabrous dawn

Woke birds and the house. Crops and the threatened war,
The evil milk laws, then his distant youth,
Building the line, and the Homeric poacher.

He was the boy who wrestled rural Goliath,
The tricky hedger, thatcher of solid name,
The fiery preacher, tireless sifter of truth.

His liver had killed him next year when I came.
The house was sold and the mares, the pleasant holding
Falling to fallow, his fame thinning to dream.

Already he was recalled as mean, and lusting
For girls and sugar, a hypocrite, dying boasting.

The Tramp

Dirtying the joy of the returning exile
At the hemlock lane falling from the crest,
He rises like conscience or the paternal call;

Lolling face, tufted by tangled waste,
Round as balloon painted with mouth and eyes
Deflates a grin above a woollen chest.

Negroid lips split and eyes glitter two ways,
The paint becomes alive, like blood under dirt,
The rubber features vivify with menace.

And tell the story of the mountain chart
Fastened to the otherwise worthless will
And the search postponed by an unstable heart.

Then, promising gold from the eventual spoil,
Takes conscientious pence and limps downhill.

Barbizon

Spoke the English fool at Barbizon
"Here for happiness they came
And won it, living as they would."
His pleasure yearned to sky like flame.

He would not believe happiness sought they
Ever, having rarely, hating when had,
Casting when found — then following
More bitterly for loss, until death.
Human, they got no more felicity
Than you, or I, or even foolish he.

Snow in London

All day from the east slanted snow
Covering pavement toys and the metal men
Who speak for England the lead laws of ago.

The ugly and the best-unseen were strewn
With white's illusion, and the brittle clocks
Cracked in the silence of an air of stone.

Rank through the noon was smell of beeves and cocks
Slain for the Child and gleaming in the eye
Like fishes nestling in the island rocks.

Beauty was white but poor man's bitter day
To tempt the tongue and soak the thinning shoe
That walks to heaven by the neon way.

Griming the white of time's unstable flow,
Man's shame survived the judgements of the snow.

Buntingsdale Revisited

Beyond the green mill where the loon was caught,
The wall a vixen leaped, our summer house of experiments
In physiology and verse confronts me on this hill —
The same, yet shrunken in a world shaped like the past.

The view is mean. The tall panorama of boyhood
Has died to its earth and trees. Standing, I remember —
Deliberately — our grandiose names of ditches.
The path is Appian. The wall of China. The grey summer house

Arthurian Camelot. But the words ring in their truth
No longer. The valley is small and the stream
Tainted with sewage. The crowded woods are ugly
And the better trees, like men, are marked for death.

Already the saw's whip crackles down the hill
And mock blood of sawdust pales anemone earth,
Where the Black Wood of Merlin is falling down
Over the ears of my remembered past.

There stand a boy and an old man beside me,
And I am both, yet am between and neither.
The boy has wasted within me, yet is unmourned;
Within me the old man grows, yet is unborn.

I am not angry at the stripping saw
Nor time that tears, for this is not my valley.
I go, the old man hanging on my back.
The boy I leave to weep on his own ruin.

Merthyrmawr

Sunday evening. The thick-lipped men binoculared
Steal through the geometric groves of pines
Observing the steady and fatal hands of poachers
And the young loving in wrinkles of the dunes.

Grey in the wind sand tides against the turrets,
And watchful sight is bridged towards the sea,
Where silent the marram defends a wearing land
And the seagulls climb like Junkers a plaster sky.

The air is alive with voices, the loving whisper,
The rodent screams at neck-constricting hand,
Gulls' earthless wail and dank watcher's laughter.
Always the wind whistles through teeth of sand.

Night falls on the lovers, marram and voices.
Dark hinders eyes, yet aids the brutal hand.
Watchers depart, but the snares are filling.
Wind dries the blood on the moving sand.

November

The days grow dim. Melancholy chrysanthemums
Wilt under dank shrubberies where roses
Still open, niggardly, to the winter sun
Cramped flowers like slum women's faces.

Traditional Sundays falling on villages
Set the harmonium measure, tea at the manse;
Song and the thudding of darts at the public,
Dark empty lanes returning from the dance.

The farmer walks home drunk across his acres
Beneath whose hedges rabbits and virgins scream,
And the uniformed shadows darken in corners,
Putting to time the riddle of their doom.

Dawseye

On risky leads, stiff to the wind of height,
    I see the known town as the roosting bird
Clutching interstices of stones would, or the bat
    Over the sky jerked, toy on a snatching cord.

Kestrel to roofs, cats' eyries, drops the sight
    And houses chasming streets for walking eyes
Sees stunted under height, till distance levels
    Town to a wrinkled floe of tiles and trees,

Walls tops that once secretly enclosed
    Imagined gardens and the fields marooned,
Detects the spinsters sunning, dogs at love,
    The vicar reading, supine on pious ground,

And stones, erupted virtues from the dead
    Marring grass as carious teeth of shark
Counts, where the pairs of faithful living men
    Foreshortened, knobbed and legless bodies, walk.

But earth too far, the vertiginous fear
    Blurs sight and wilful as a weight
Drags down until the queasy eyes return
    Where falling stairs twirl, friendly to my feet.

Reading Tolstoy

Now Levin drinks the water flecked with rust
and in my mouth a bitter tang of iron
draws flat. Rabbits lived then; their sandy warren
grew mushrooms big as plates; dark in own dusk
the oakwood clambered down its red soft cliff
and stuck its feet of alder deep in bog.
In that sour sedge once woodcocks came to dig
with long pronged totem bills and stiff
steps angular. They fled in lumbering zigzags.
Whether I saw those rare dark namesake birds,
as once bright hoopoe high on Alpine road,
or made a myth from small snipes' stilted legs,
I know no more. But see the marsh return,
the birds in problem shadows strutting, brass
blaring of kingcups down the dank morass,
and dense beneath the cliff a nest of fern
where crystal out of green the spring jets forth
and fills the small tin cup whose taste wakes in my mouth.

First Spring on the Island

Our first spring on that island. Other strangers
had prospered there, but now the land was sick,
worked out and overgrown with broom and alder.
Still, every day, alone, I'd take the track
down from the trailer in among the firs
and hack down broom. Broom petals, winter honey,
dripped on my sweaty arms. The limping killdeer
cried through the grass in wing-drag mockery
and garter snakes whipped sliding brown from blade
beyond death's accident — till in that knot
of blue-eyed grass one turned to coil and sway,
struck venomless and bit upon my boot,
that small head jabbing vainly at its hardness.
I held death's poisoned fang that day. I struck
with rage and loathing, struck again, again —
most madly mashed his body with my stick
and dropped its pulp among the sky-tinged flowers.
Twelve years ago, but deathless in the brain,
a snake's strange courage, and my human shame.

Victorian Custom

Grasping the barrel,
within season of course,
you pulled a shotgun,
loaded and cocked
through a quick hedge,
across a stone fence.
A thorn
or a rock edge
tipped the trigger,
blew your side in.
It was almost a
Victorian custom.
Speke of the Nile
did it
to avoid facing Burton,
and my great-grandfather,
Thomas Woodcock
to avoid facing
a roomful of daughters
without dowries.

Juries of sportsmen
returned appropriate verdicts.
They knew
in those days
that life also
is mainly accidental.

Silent Hounds Loping

The night
drifts into your forest
and the cry
grows faint.
The hounds are silent
loping towards you,
old hunter, dying.

Seeing another forest
where the hounds waited,
hunter and warrior
tonight you weep;
with old man's tears
wash time away.
A lost front, a lost war
drowned under six decades of history
rises to you out of memory.

We stand beside you
under the pine trees
and the night waits
for chance to speak,
the enemy unseen.
You, and that boy you see
with such choking memory,
crawl through the heath and fern
into the night
that breaks with noise and light.

Then through the light he falls
in night for ever,
and you
hacked deep by lead
survive to nurse your wounds
and not forget.
Holding your hand
in the instant of hallucination
I become your comrade.
You weep for me also.

Old mountaineer
you stand
at the white saddle
on your way down
from the blinding peak
where you have seen
guides and companions
fall past you into space,
you helpless.
It is all memory
but for you as real
as your delirium
and for us as real
as your tears falling
bright as if frozen
into the dark crevasse
where the men you survive
and the beasts you slaughtered
wait.

The Wolves Depart

We have attended too often
the theatre of your dying
when you have cried
all the wolves of the continent,
the gaunt survivors from
Transylvanian forests and
Pyrennean gullies, standing
hungry and fire-eyed
to howl the chorus as you
wept and lamented
the grey next morning
when we would not find
you alive — and each morning
you greeted us
smiling and
forgetful.

But now the theatre is closed and
the wolves gone
to other hauntings;
it has been established
they are not man-eaters.

I find you
speechless, your eyes
glowing with a dumb wonder,
and feel, as you do,
another predator
silently drawing near
on feline
inescapable
pads.

The Geomantic Dragon

Turning black mould
under the oak tree
in the garden corner
where we had dug
often
and found nothing
it was you encountered
the dragon.

From a great vessel
by dead fingers made,
a splinter sharp as a knife,
and as we washed
the lines
faint and cerulean
emerged out of greyness,
Chinese cloud arcs
and sailing through them
the magic reptile,
wings, tail and horns
complete, fire-breathing,
self-magnifying.

Was this the being,
true landlord, lord of lands,
protector geomantic
who rang clear bells
in old house corners
and when we worked
through the night's depth
sent odour of violets,
cakes and stables
seeping fresh
from place's past,
benevolent?

Was this he,
tired of speaking
to ear and nostril,
taking new form
to offer through eye
and fingertip
validation of our life,
and the best years of a lifetime
spent in this garden,
green well of shadow,
under the giant cherry
whose eighty years' abundance
feeds wasps and robins,
flickers, raccoons
and other friends
less animal and wise,

and white enfolds
in spring
the house you also
discovered
on your first meeting —
unaware then —
with the dragon
who compelled your choice
and now offers
his image in blue lines
on the fragment of a vessel
made by some old Chinese,
eye and hand wise
and, like yourself,
shaper of forms,
a potter?

Dragon king
of unknown provenance
unexpected arrival
and undoubted
Taoist allegiance,
accept this invocation,
bless our life
within your guarded land
with love and
dragon's gifts,
the power to change,
to grow in the
fluidity transforming
eternal dark to light.

November Day
on Howe Sound

The best of all Novembers
as the mountains shout
when that low-slanted sun
lights them from within,
igniting from grey stone
alchemic vividness:
vermilion, rust, fire orange,
viridian, copper-blue,
faded Prussian, moss
green, arbutus bronze.

Rock slide and mountain wall
glistening in cascade spray:
at level-rayed evening
exploding into gold:
in autumn fire haze
distancing amethyst.

Last leaves burn on trees
stripped to bone of life
or dance down wind,
bright dying butterflies
asserting mortal splendour
at the year's end of life
framed by the glistening
indifferent sea.

O mountains shout again
and gold leaves die in flight
on that bright day you
sing me into night.

Souvenir of Cambodia

1. *The Woman on the Treadmill*

Kampong Chhnang
where the hills end
and the marshes begin.
The sky burning blue
and behind the town
a blue lagoon among
jade paddies and
buffalo meadows.

A woman treads a
watermill; conical
mushroom of hat,
dirty brown sampot
down to her heels,
she holds her bar
and tramps in the noon
sun, and the water
rises in bamboo
buckets and spills
in diamond flashes
into her paddy.

We see her
and are gone,
but I know her
image will stay
in my mind. I
shall remember
as I do now
the image
of a land.

2. Ta Prohm, near Angkor Wat

This was a temple
they did not free
from the jungle.
The air under the trees
is sullen, breathless,
but the forest clatters
with life, insects
trilling, jungle
cocks crowing, copper-
smiths tapping, and
ficus trees stand
on the wall and
send down their roots
like pythons,
crushing and prising
until the stones
fall into moraines
and the roofs
collapse and let
the light in.

Gigantic bats
rustle and shit
in the empty chambers.
There is a smell
of civet. Snake skins
flutter like limp
cellophane, the monkeys
call in the trees,
the spiders
sit in great funnels
of gossamer.

Yet in the heart
of the maze
a broken tower
and the sun falling
on a broken
Buddha
and a rusty tin
filled with the burntout
ends of joss-sticks.

We search
for that last
hermit
in vain.

3. Pnom Penh: The Diamond Bowler

Sweet sounds of
gongs and strings
over the palace
compound. The
Royal Dancers
are rehearsing in
their gilded crowns.
We are not allowed
to Peer. The
Queen Mother
is observing.

Instead we may gape
at the royal jewels,
at the coronation crowns,
one for the throne, one
for the palanquin, one
for horseback, one for
elephant driving;
at the throne and the
bed of state and
the two mats for washing,
gold for the right foot,
silver for the left;
at the funeral chariot
and the golden basket for
washing the royal ashes
in coconut milk;
at the black bowler
bought in Bond Street
with a ruby knob
set by the palace jeweller
on the crown,
and on the side a
cockade with a
forty-carat diamond
focussing
east with west.

Mythology

Metaurus

Proud with his pachyderms filing the perilous passes
brought Barca Romeward fear and bleak danger
dire of arson and fire mouths feeding on riches,
corrosion of famine, ravishment of the nubile, terror
of arrows at noon, swords in the dark, blood
on the oak leaves, on the reeds of Arno,
terror of trodden flowers, of dust to strange feet stirring
out of Capua, of eagles broken, emblems annihilated.

Fire in the veins, a furnace in the reins,
burning a pyre of pride across the brain,
Trebia to Trasimene triumph ran like fire!
Cannae's fulfilment! In an enemy land
Victory! Victory in the garden of Rome!

But weak eyes after, in hostile hills
marches to terror of ambush, watches
on bare peninsulas, sleepless camps,
signals from cliffs, the mirages of rumour,
over the palisades the head hurled, agony
of recognition by firelight, message of Metaurus
said by dry lips, visions in carrion eyes
of goalless marches, nightfalls of defeat,
starved tongues, the flight from oasis to desert,
the chase narrowing, the dead whispering,
the lipped cup opening immortality.

Panegyric

Who the pass sold to the invading ant
 And sky surrendered to the hornet swarm,
Sacks the wardrobe for the critical moth
 And barks the log for the recalcitrant worm.

The mantis gesture, claws concealed in prayer,
 Veils his armament of explosive speech.
The phosgene sigh and the barbed gesture wait
 Under the skin for the kinetic scratch.

The glycerine tear swells from the rubber duct
 At squirrels' depredations, the waxed voice
Lips regretful formulae, saving face,
 But promises the plundered no redress.

So, when the guns snap in the nearest field
 He hears, as adders in a drying well,
But still pursues the avenues of guile,
 Advising isolation's magic wall.

Odysseus

Odysseus, returning home in state,
Discharged some standing debts, swept out his home,
Handed out presents of exotic things
And, taking off his shoes, went up to bed.
Time having tightened in the weft's last thread,
He and Penelope were one again.

The Island

The oars fell from our hands. We climbed the dark
    Slopes of kelp to the stairway up the rock.
Scott went first, grasping the fraying rope.
    The rest of us followed, dragging the iron rack.

The crest was bare, but after a scanty search
    In a bird's burrow we found the hunted man.
His flesh was naked and hard as barren earth,
    His arms like scythes. His eyes spoke like a gun.

Before him we retired, unmanned by fear.
    Unarmed, he seemed to move with harmful light.
Scott only stood, shaming us in the end.
    The fugitive surrendered without fight.

We laid him on the painful rack, stretched tight
    His limbs and bound his feet and wrists with wire,
Set leaden weights upon his sunken chest
    And tied his head down by the matted hair.

We turned the cranks and wrenched him hour by hour.
    In silence he endured. He would not speak
Of the hidden ore. At last his joints burst out
    And jetting from the ruptures fire broke.

Then lay before us on the rigid rack
    Straw limbs and a horse's polished skull.
Gulls mocked as walked away across the sea
    The man we hunted but could not keep or kill.

We threw the rack into the hungry surf
    And hacked the turf in anger with our swords.
Then re-embarking on our fruitless voyage,
    We left the island to the mice and birds.

Gods

That was the plain, where grass instead of hair
    Grew on the heads of gods, whose temples stood
Phallic and gleaming in the vast morass
    Held from its hunger by great rafts of wood.

At night the gods went in their iron trucks
    Along the causeways, paved with frozen flesh
And built on cubes of papier-maché rock.
    Into the villages beyond the marsh.

There they were offered nails and human teeth,
    Foreskins and crutches of the grateful lame.
Virginities were broken on their knees.
    The village feuds were started in their name.

But through all this the gods impassive sat.
    The wheels that bowed their heads and moved their jaws,
Had long been rusty and their limbs were set
    Hard as their own outdated changeless laws.

Dies Irae

When the guardians of the sacred pools
    Slew the holy carp and fled to sea
He spoke the fears of the faithful poor,
    Foretelling God's rage for that bitter day.

Galled by the laughter of the sceptic rich,
    He ripped his threadbare gown and scooped up mud
To crown his baldness, howling like a wolf,
    Shouting incendiary images of the mad.

Fearing his threat of the revolting slum,
    The senate granted that pursuit was just,
Outlawed the culprits and summoned all true men
    To hang them from the rooftree or the mast.

Homing triumphant by the sacred pools,
    He saw the dead shoal gleaming on the ground,
Thought of his starving women and their brats,
    And stole the largest with a righteous hand.

For an Elder Statesman

Fishing beside the ends of choked canals,
  He did not know Troy fallen, Lenin dead;
Only the swing of seasons did he feel,
  Petals to leaves to snowflakes on his head.

And, after death, subaqueous heavens him held
  And dank havens of his earthly wish,
Sunk in the glory of eternal gloom,
  One with Christ, the elemental fish.

Ballad of an Orphan Hand

Orphan the hand that made the bell
Toll in tower lost had father,
Brother, kin, body and arm.
Warm the sun and keen the air
Were the fosterers of that hand
And watched his journeys through the land.

Hand's life was easy, duty small.
All feared his presence lest some ill
Fall, and gave him dues of fear.
Far was he known, most in repute.
Few knew the goodness of that hand
Landing so neatly on wall or ground.

Carrying rope for the rash,
Cash for the needy, a flower
For the neglected, a stone
When evil offended, the unseen hand
Sent his boons with skilful throw
Over the wall, through the window.

So he was mostly anonymous,
As when his games were taken for ghosts',
Gifts for elf's kindness. He did not kill
While fear slew fools, stole only from rich,
Which is not stealing. Indeed, of sin
One only had he, and that women.

Hand could resist no female charm,
Arm soft and fat, full amorous breast,
Fast palpitating, or nubile thigh
Sighing for fondling in empty room
Tempted hand's lascivious touch
Towards the dark piscian arch.

To many he appeared in sleep,
Slipping like snake between the clothes,
Raising the garment like a dream.
Came to others as the wind
Round the damp limbs at cloying dusk,
Risking discovery at amorous task.

Favoured the women, lovely and few
Who knew hand's fingers like feet of prince
Prance on the cill or round the door,
Soar like bird to the waiting herd,
Led as lover to lecherous night
Lit by ardour of their delight.

But one the woman whose lust of hand
Ended for ever his freedom and love.
Craving always that silver touch,
Rash in absence she plotted to keep,
Captured by stealth too eager hand,
And caged in a box to enjoy without end.

But freedom is sweeter than love, and hand
Ended in hating each lecherous day.
Faded his skin like a lightless plant,
And shrank his flesh till fingers were bone.
Then hand, with a bitter wish for the sky,
Died like a whore for lechery.

The Hero

Out of the east the hero came,
tall as a tree and swift as a flame,
lithe as water and lovely as cream.

But his eyes were fire and his tongue was steel,
his finger a flag and his voice a bell
and magic to rats and men his will.

He slew the kings and the titled drones,
felled the chapels and gods of stone
and made his roads with the sacred bones.

He used his guns to bring down rain,
fed the poor with the royal grain,
killed the church and the dread of thirteen.

But he died, and they buried his bones in gold,
his laws were frozen in a changeless code
and his name was God on the lips of the old.

Till another hero came from the east
and threw his bones for the dogs to feast.

The Return of Odysseus

Poor was the village and wet the way
When X. came back last Easter Day.

Scant was the food and thin the beer
When X came back with his comrade Fear.

Strange were the kids and the old men daft
When X returned like an empty craft.

The women went white and screamed of a ghost
When X came limping in from the coast.

And the wrestlers shuddered in church and house
When X returned to his home and spouse.

The clock was striking, the hour was fate,
When X came in at the garden gate.

Time was failing, the end was sure
When X was knocking the kitchen door.

The spouse went mad, the other went dumb,
When X stood there from kingdom come.

For the house was full and full the bed
When X returned from the far and the dead.

But he was lame and he was blind,
X moaning there in the bitter wind,

And unseen the face, unknown the way
When X came back that Easter Day.

So they gave him pence and gave him food
And set his face on the inland road,

And time restarted, the men went sane
When X walked on in the wind and rain.

The Old King

The old king returned from evenings on the sand
Unknown and happy in a salty land
Between the vineyards and the era's end,
A dotard leaving love and the kind hand.

Foe of no fog or any striking steel
Was his return to ordered act and will
In his unhappy city on the hill
Of loveless eyes and hands that dared not heal.

But in the veins and organs in the ear
The voices freed him from the walls, and far
The golden beaches where the nightly fear
Wrapped like a love round tamarisk and tear.

And in the coil of that objecting heart
Struck like a thorn time's unastounding hurt.
The crumpled body in a dirty cart
Came from a land where vineyards scurf with salt.

Imagine the South

Imagine the South from which these migrants fled,
Dark-eyed, pursued by arrows, crowned with blood,
Imagine the stiff stone houses and the ships
Blessed with wine and salt, the quivering tips
Of spears and edges signalling in the sun
From swords unscabbarded and sunk in brine,
Imagine the cyclamen faces and yielding breasts
Hungered after in a dead desert of icy mists,
Imagine, for though oblivious, you too are cast
Exile upon a strange and angry coast.

Going into exile away from youth,
You too are losing a country in the south,
Losing, in the red daylight of a new shore
Where you are hemmed by solitude and fear,
The loving faces far over a sea of time,
The solid comfort and the humane dream
Of a peaceful sky, the consoling patronage
And the golden ladder to an easy age;
All these are lost, for you too have gone away
From your Southern home upon a bitter journey.

There is no home for you marked on the compass.
I see no Penelope at the end of your Odysseys,
And all the magic islands will let you down.
Do not touch the peaches and do not drink the wine,
For the Dead Sea spell will follow all you do,
And do not talk of tomorrow, for to you
There will only be yesterday, only the fading land,
The boats on the shore and tamarisks in the sand
Where the beautiful faces wait, and the faithful friends.
They will people your mind. You will never touch their hands.

Ferdinand Lassalle

His past was always with him. In his blood
He carried the messenger with the poisoned knife
Ready to gash his brain and drain his heart.
The speaking statue attended all his triumphs.

Down the soft Rhineland roads and through the shouts
Of little German towns he rode with garlands,
The leader of an age, the good disciple
Who stole his teacher's credit for his own.

He was audacious and a people loved him.
His lameness was the perpetual memento.
His triumph ran through the heart of Germany.
Death's triumph ran through his rotting heart.

The messenger led him, one summer morning,
To the empty field on the edge of the city
Where time was waiting with words of lead.
He died and Marx rejoiced at his dying.

Breughel

Snow falls in ash across a smoky sky.
The dun-clad hunters, crossing a white valley,
Follow the compass noses of their hounds
To the bare copse on the little pointed hills.

The crisp air colours their lined, cunning faces,
Intent on the end of the hunt and the genial evening
Swilling in the dirty straw of a welcome hovel.
Thus they will consume the slow years to senility.

Thus they will cross the narrow valleys of days,
Following the quarry perennial and elusive,
Until one evening they enter a closed valley
And, finding no outlet and the entrance drift-bound,

Sink into the snow sleep of death.
Looking upon their moment set in paint,
Held up from death by hands long laid away,
I see our future mirrored in their past,

The long and fruitless days on cold landscapes,
The quiet hills, deceptive valleys of love,
And the unnamed quarry eluding every chase,
Until the last hunt clogs our eyes with snow.

The Fugitive

The stranger leant on his door, and through his window
The enemy eyes of stars burnt into his sleep.
Surrounded by foes, plucking his fear about him,
He dreamed desperately of a friendly future.

He saw the quiet bodies and empty eyes
That carried no treason. He saw enormous forests
Where races could vanish, and the far lovely islands
Divided by turbulent seas from the fearful mainland.

He saw the ice pyramid where the naked Yogin
Entered a solitary and impersonal heaven.
He saw the gardens hanging on ultimate cliffs
And the lovers alone and together over a distant sea.

But over all the journeys of his dreams
The hostile stars looked with their million eyes,
And his travels ended in that sleepless city
Where all men watched him, all women were false and bland.

The Agitator

The yellow flowers broken by his feet
Sent up their acrid warning to his heart;
The wordless signpost like a rotting tongue
Gave him no answer, and he had no chart

Written upon his mind, behind the eyes.
The thickets where the clear-voiced blackcap sang,
The little sedge-trimmed pools between the trees
Led him to a new country where his foes were strong.

Somewhere at the end there lay a city
Where the women would greet him in their smoky houses,
Holding the knife hidden within the girdle
Or offering slow venom in coloured beautiful glasses.

And in that city he must reject their cunning,
Outwit the foxy men who watched his step
And carry his doctrine quietly in his heart
Until the hour when daily thought would stop,

Crowds would see visions, and his thoughts, like birds
Burdened with messages, would find their homes.
Already in mind he saw the breasts of men
Opening to free the phoenix of their dreams.

The little hills that lay along his path
Shed their long shadows as the evening fell.
Beyond their wall, west by the setting sun,
The paper gunmen waited for their kill.

Portrait

Do you remember the old gentleman? The imitator
Of forgotten Gods, appearing in four disguises —
The living skeleton, the almost legendary ancestor,
The thin devil and angel with four faces.

He was a believer in the intimate touch.
A craftsman always. In the appropriate deed
An artist often, felicitous to catch
The ultimate gesture or angle of the head.

Some feared him. To many he was a friend
Welcome at the end of a long wait
Or appearing suddenly in the nick of time.
He liked the dark and carried his own night.

You may not have seen him lately. He's more careful
Now, being nervous of streets and mercury light,
And does not travel so much, because of age.
But he's very far from finished, whatever you thought.

Some day one of his multichromatic eyes
Will spy you, as he steps from the swimming pool
Or jumps from behind the bean vines or over the sill,
And you, like the others, will answer his syren call.

Poem

Leaves on her back,
Ideas in her hair,
The dead girl sleeps among us,
Her worms are long and fair.

Her white breasts are falling
In devastated domes.
Under their soft shelter
We had our dreams.

Flower lips have withered
Snarling on carious teeth.
Touch that gave glory
Shocks with cold death.

The dead girl sleeps among us.
Who dare claim her night?
Carry her into the quiet earth.
Her rotten bones are light.

Look Away from the Lake

Look away from the lake and the skaters
Into the forest where the young men lie
Glazed into columns or pierced by ice arrows,
Their horses huddled under shrouds of snow.

On a May morning they rode out of yesterday
Following the ventriloquial cuckoo.
The road they travelled was submerged in roses,
The land they crossed sunk under seas of beauty.

They went without kissing their weeping women.
Their eyes were bright, their songs were peasant and soft.
They rode gaily from a land of peace and plenty
Into the unknown, they knew not where or why.

The colour of hope lay like gold on their faces.
They travelled with laughter through barren lands
Following the summer as it ebbed to the equator.
They were friendly and pleasant with the men they met,

Their guns were silent — only their money spoke
Its fiery passage into the hearts of men.
They never wanted for women or food or friends,
But always the itch in their hearts would drive them on.

Always they travelled, over the sunny roads
And through the parched plains and the wooded hills.
The elusive bird flew ever before them
Into the dark forests where tomorrow lurked.

Here they wandered long in obscure shadows.
The bird had left them and the summer gone
Towards the antipodes of their desire.
Dark winter found them in the twilight forest.

Dark winter found them and their journey ended.
In the freezing forest they found and knew their purpose.
The snow drifted over their closing nostrils
As they reached their goal and grail in death.

The King's Grave

Noon lay I in grave's green cup
Bedded and lapped by lips of loam,
Naked I, weary on tumulus turf
Threw my jeers at the daft pale sky,
Whose pinchback clouds and pregnant sun
Span like toys and danced my tune.

Breast of earth the grave me bedding
Prisoned the man beneath my back,
Dead and rotten beneath my living,
Bone and dust for the jealous marl,
Perch for the coiling worm and the root,
Three thousand still years of kingship's fruit.

Bare skull eyeless domes a void,
Femurs stain and crack in frost,
Damp splits the green and rusting swords,
And only the earthen pots are whole.
Leaders revert to soil and lime.
Cups they lip are spared in time.

So my spreadeagle of careless body
Crucified in supine of ease
To taunt the sun and flannel heaven
Cringes over the parallel dead.
Now in the May pluck of full life
I know the warning, soiling wave.

To dust the sounding psalm impels
Me as imperial cage of ribs
Close in the dank plebeian clay,
As midge that dies between my palms,
As all life crumbling into slime,
Dissolving under dusk's decline.

Listening to the viscous air
I hear the future's echo sound
Faint, but growing like a dome,
Wordless, but warning to the strong.
For, meagre or Caesarian their ends,
All men are sucked beneath the same sure sands.

Arctic Death

High in the grey, and golden gyrating,
Osprey and eagle wheeled above those
Blond explorers whom northern autumn
Closed in and caught too late for leaving.

Hare's fur blanched, marsh slime set granite,
Bushes burnt crimson, charred grey for winter;
All game had gone, by stealth retreating
To tree lines provident with lichen.

Too long they'd waited along the traplines.

So in bleak barren, tempest-bitten,
Bivouacs built, a wealth of corpses —
Fox and marten in wall-width morticed,
Matted fine furs in aspic winter.

There chewed raw fish, shrugged cold, despaired,
Yawned in the daze of snow, and slept;
Like silver kings in that locked north
Waited the sweet, corrupting spring.

Revisionist Legend One

I do not know
who was Jocasta's
father (though that
would be easy to find)
but seeing you,
untouched by your own hand
mourning Oedipus
who broke the legend
(dying before you
and unblinded),
I look into your doe's
dark hunted eyes
and being, as they say,
quite old enough to be
your father, I imagine
how Jocasta's father
loved his daughter,
and suspecting that the sphinx
to stir up trouble
gave the wrong answers,
I am drained with sadness
until the sparkling tears
waken your eyes,
provoke my longing.

Revisionist Legend Two

I let you down, of course,
doubly, watching
your heels kick at the
tipped-up stool, but
staying alive, and also
unblinded, even
unblinkered. It has been
a clarification and
a freeing.

Remember, I was the ignorant
coming in off the road
with blood on my hands.
You, having heard the
prophecy, knew and savoured
revenge's rankness, when that
self-grown instrument which
fate returned
both killed and cuckolded
your enemy, my father.

There were always tears. Ours
was a necessary union, destined
not happy,
from the moment you
designed dementia
in palace corridors and
I came upon you, weeping and
naked, wandering.

There was more afterwards
when I turned to the young ones.
Jabbed by jealousy
the ghost then
rose in your nightmare.
There was struggle
at the barred doors, shouting
of river and rope,
and guards gossiping
in the town.

One day, even
in the interests of state,
it was inevitable
my hand should cease
restraining.
If letting die is
murder,
I am your murderer;
if upsetting the prophecy
is hubris
the gods are my enemies.
But, unblinding myself, I
see the deities in their
chthonian burrows
as earth,
necessity from which we
rise — and above!

Letting unreason die
makes reason triumph;
one becomes oneself by
renewing the
father murdered, and
one's realm is
undivided
until the next
cycle begins,
below
        Delphi
                at the
                        Crossroads

What Did Merlin Say?

At the gate to the dark wood
what did Merlin say
to the king's sister
Morgan-le-Fay?

"Little fox, remember
that the lion and the lamb
can lie down together
and the fox and the hare
be at peace in the heather,
yet in the world's nature
as God makes the creature,
the lion chews no cud,
the lamb drinks no blood,
and the fox and the hare
no issue can share
in form or in lair
and Nebuchadnezzar
eating grass
is a twisting of rightness
that must pass.

"For magic may speak
and changes wreak
that shake God's proportion,
but change is only
the petals that open
in the secret rose.
The heart of the rose
is still
as the prism rotates.
Becoming
is the luminous motion
of being
which moves not.

"And always God's balance
settles again
on the long slow way
for foxes and queens
of peace and pain
in the valley enisled
at Avalon."

So spoke sage Merlin
to Morgan-le-Fay
on the way to Avalon
at the end of that long-dusked
Cymric day.

And no man knows
what answer gave
the little fox
or the queen so grave.

The Outlaw Exonerated

*In 1906 the Gitksan Indian Gun-an-Noot was accused
of two murders, and fearing racial bias in his trial,
fled into the wilderness north of the Skeena. For
thirteen years, often shadowing his hunters, but never
harming them, he remained at large. He was never
captured, but surrendered voluntarily in 1919, stood
trial and was acquitted. He returned, spirit broken,
to his hunting life, and died in the wilderness in 1933.
A mountain was named after him.*

Simon Gun-an-Noot
walked out of freedom
into justice.
A jury condemned him;
A jury acquitted him.
Did that even the score?
Did it balance
the thirteen years
of flight and exile?
Did it make him any more
innocent? Did it
liberate him? He was
innocent and free already.

The voices of manmade law
claimed virtue and merit
for releasing this outlaw,
but the outlaw lived
in another law;
the law of nature, not
to kill without reason,
not to waste life like
polluted water.

In the wild distances
beyond systems, beyond
codes and courthouses,
lie the heart's solitudes
where life is sucked from
the sands of adversity
and wisdom's a thirst
quenched only by those
who lose their worlds
and find their own beings.

And wisdom is madness
before it is joy.
The stones of the courthouse
set Gun-an-Noot free,
but his heart was sad
and his sadness a burden
carried back to the Skeena,
to trapline and trading,
not young any longer,
and marked by loneness,
claimed by the bush.

Simon Gun-an-Noot
escaped once again
from life into peace.
They buried him
by a green lake
in the far beyond
and called a mountain
Gun-an-Noot.

The Skeena

The Skeena
is the river of mists.
It flows out of the dark heart
of the west, out
of the wilds of
Omineca, the lands
the white man has passed
through and partly ravaged,
the lands now abandoned,
known only to the
last hunters.

The Skeena
flows from mountains
through mountains,
the lordly massif of
Rocher Déboulé, the
clustering heads
of the Seven Sisters,
a parade of snow crowns
marching to the edge
of ocean, and
the river flowing,
fast, broad, brown
between stone drifts
and bleached log jams,
forests golden of
spring and of winter.

On these slow reaches
ghosts of steamboats
and shouting captains
call in the distance
of history, but
no ship now weathers
whirlpools and races
and Skeena flows in
primeval silence
or shouts
to itself as
it struggles whitely
through the long canyon
by the stones of Kitselas
where the Tsimshian chiefs,
clansmen of Stoneface,
trading in from the coast
brought great canoes
carved by Haida, coloured
and crested and
heavy with fish oil,
to be dragged on kelp ropes
through boiling waters
to the upper river,
domain of Temleham,
home of the inland
hunters, the
Gitksan, the
river's people.

On these high reaches
of the river of mists,
and by the tributaries
that seep from grey mountains,
goat-peopled Stekyawden
and the magic foothills
of Temleham
where men lived
immortal and rich
until they derided
the animal spirits,
the kings of salmon,
lords of the
mountain goats,
and were sent like Adam
to worlds of dying:
among these dark waters
the Gitksan
seeded villages,
named them
for their own lineages:
Kitwanga, Kitwancool,
Kitsequecla, Kisgegas,
Kitanmax, Kispiox, Qaldo.
In these places
they lived in their houses,
Wolf and Eagle,
Raven and Fireweed;
remembering ancestors
in legend's distance
they built great houses
of spruce and cedar
above young rivers
where salmon struggled
leaping for life,

spawning into
the red brightness
of death.

The houses were painted
with crests and emblems,
the encounters with spirits
that made chiefs noble.
Each house was entered
through its needle eye,
hole in a great post
that spelt clan myths
in the tongue of symbols,
figures that clamber,
beasts and men,
to the shaman's heaven.

A grove made by men
before the great houses:
towering totems,
by carving heraldic,
by painting magic,
raised with feasting,
dancing and boasts
of chiefs in
bird masks, in
ermine, blankets of
goat's wool, eagle's down
spilling from crowns
of sealion whiskers
with glittering seashell
on brows iridescent,
and each man ranked
in the eye of custom,
graded and graded
to infinite levels,

no two equal and
each man knowing
his place at the potlatch
where great giving
exalted the giver,
shamed the receiver
till he too gave.
Giving, receiving,
giving again;
asserting rank,
each man's place
in the eye of
the circling sun.

It was the heart
in the world of
the Gitksan,
river's people.
It was the blood
of their art, pulse
of their fellowship.

And so they lived
till the white men came;
the world was changed
and a sun
fell from the sky.

Kreutzer Sonata

Tolstoy at least
did not fear
making a fool of himself
over sex. He knew
the cock-and-cunt game
inside and upward,
lamented his wrinkled
and drained innocence,
called on the young
to keep their dreams dry
and defend their privities.

He went on fucking
and came in words.

Ploughing Pastures

Pivoting on the autumn farm
Swing gulls come inland, boding storm
Like white ambassadors of harm.

Swollen from dots they seem afar,
Gulls spiral down the gusty air,
Long glide, white flicker when earth's near.

One hillside draws them, like the dead
Attracting vultures, to its red
Tilth like raw flesh open laid.

For on that field where I have seen
The valley seasons one by one
Come and grow full and wane,

A tractor drawing ruthless blades
Tears up old grass and pleasant weeds
To bed the spring's more fruitful seeds,

And on the sillion white birds fall
With flutter of wing and rip wind brawl
To snatch with golden tearing bill

The helpless life the share upturns,
Slow, earth-living, groping worms,
And inert larvae, flight's first forms.

So this favourite land is cleft,
This ancient turf that held my weight
Ripped by blades that slice like fate,

And so the fallow of my life
Splits to this hour's implacable knife
As autumn burns the day and leaf,

And iron beaks tear from the heart
Latent feeling and larval thought
And every love that grows for flight.

But this dear field in distant June
Like health's regenerated skin
Will crowd with barley's swaying green,

And all its scar be covered up
By greater beauty, richer hope.
So may my peace outgrow time's rape.

Eagle

Down the cliff's edge, high on a leaning cedar
Whose branches hang in drooping deprecation,
Quietly resigned, as if mourning desolation
Left by the petulant saw and brutal tractor,
An eagle sits like the poet's conquistador,
Erect and peering through the lifting mist
Haughtily towards Japan and the ominous East.
This is a conqueror who seeks no glory, nor
The smoky golden loot of distant lands.
His eye slopes over, not beyond the ocean,
Seeks the betraying ripple, form above sand
Refracted through slack water, trembling fin.
Then on wide wings he falls, a shabby terror,
And ragged hunger breaks the sea, his mirror.

Deer

A dog barks in the distance. A moment later
Delicately through the sword fern steps the buck,
Polished prongs high, tense ears, his fear
Dwindling as he stops in the old cart track
To nibble the amethyst daisies between the ruts.
A dry crack in the wood; he pauses an instant,
Tapestry beast among the python roots
Of the giant fir-trees, tawny against the jet
Charred Christ-year stump. A dead branch falls
And he leaps away like a northern kangaroo,
Plunges in the glossy darkness of salal
As the bluejays scream in derision to see him go.
Lord, preserve him from the pitlamper's greed,
Avert the hunter's fury, the cougar's leap.

The Game Shop in Colmar

The shop front is Art Nouveau,
drab green, with the word GIBIER
gold on a foxed mirror,
and iron hooks welded
to an iron bar
over the window.
Draggled bunches of hares
and pheasants
hang limp as rags,
so unlike themselves
that I forget the buck hare
I watched with joy last night
on a moonlit road's edge,
cavorting among the cabbages;
forget him, and think I'll enjoy
for dinner tonight
a *hasenpfeffer*, piquant, hot.

Think, that is, until I see
those dark eyes
staring
out of the shop's depth.

The doe's head
rests on a chopping block,
but the eyes are still so bright
and sorrowful
that at first I think it a live beast,
and then, peering in,
see the severed cylinder
of brown neck
behind the alert eyes.

There is something
invincibly
human about
decapitation.
No animal can perform
such tidy severance.
I think at once
of Mary Queen of Scots
and Anne Bullen,
wondering if their eyes
looked with the same hopeless reproach
at the henchmen and headsmen
of the fierce Tudors.

Then mind flips
twenty years,
five thousand miles,
arid Guanajuato, the catacombs
whose desiccated dead
lounge in the attitudes of
an interrupted and consequently
eternal debauch,
when they are not lying in their coffins,
paralysed in the last struggle,
mouths shouting silence,
arms resisting air,
no gentle goers
into any night.
I watch them
with a defensive irony
until at the feet of these
roisterers and resisters
my eye freezes
on a head that looks severed;
no body,

a swathe of black hair
and tight mask of features,
lips retracted, empty sockets.
Young once, perhaps lovely,
like the doe in the gameshop
staring at me.

And as the mind slips back
doe and dead woman
are one,
and the iron hooks
creak under Gestapo game,
echt menschenfleisch,
wingless and two-legged
whitemeat.

Tonight, for dinner,
I eat fish.
Their blood is cold,
their eyes are coloured discs,
expressionless,
without reproach.
Even the Buddhist monks
in Thailand
eat them
without sense of sin.

Kestrel

Kestrel, bird of the middle sky,
I hesitate to address you.
The English poets turned you
into a cliché, Hopkins using you
with intellectual splendour,
Day Lewis misusing you
with politic dulness.

Yet each day, as I travel
this narrow Bavarian road
between dying villages and
see you above the same field
balancing in the lark's air,
every line curved cruelly and
necessary for your special being;
see you balanced, wings vibrating
and then out of your wind hover
plunging to your quarry,
I feel the same elation
I feel when I see horses
racing, manes streaming
around the confines of paddocks.

Your deeds are determined
by need and instinct,
yet joy is created
by your flight, by your standing
in the high air, by that
dizzying fall when your shape
and your motion are one.
Joy is liberation
within one's nature.
It is not flight
from the self.

I watch you and the paradox
of necessity and freedom
exists no more. We act
as we must, racing
in the paddocks of our destinies;
we hover and swoop in the
skies of our possibilities,
and life, like all else, is
finite yet infinite, and
joy takes us out of time
and so into freedom,
and necessity becomes
the ground of our liberation.

Fly on, kestrel, brave bird
flashing your red splendour
down the rushing air.
Your life is short and
yet your time is
endless.

Dog and Hare

A sudden squall in the green wheat
and hare leaps out, hind legs pumping,
zigzagging over the ploughland, a young
German Shepherd racing silently behind him.
They flash into the wood and like a film still
their running's image freezes in my mind
as I stay watching from the muddy footpath.

I hear the muffled tolling of the cuckoo,
see with satisfaction the line of campion
reddening the wood's edge, and watch two wild doves,
grey and glimmering as opal, parading
their beauties for each other. These
are the tenuous pleasures of the expatriate
returning to something like his childhome;
in this Bavarian landscape flora and bestiary
are those I remember from an England
I have left decisively, yet now and then,
unreasonably, regret.

But the picture
that memory asks for is not here completely.
I look in vain down the green ranks of wheat stems
for the bloody splash of poppy, the shards
of cornflower broken sky, even the scarlet,
low on the ground, of pimpernel.
None is there. Even the German bauer,
conservative, heavy with klöse, has surrendered
nature to technology. The old harmonies
of wild and cultivated, grain
for food, and flower that only feeds
the eye and spirit, are ended
for the time being.

Looking, I remember
how often on this trip I have felt a doom
suspended over Europe, as I have not
felt it for thirty years, and in houses
and gastwirtschaften I have heard men talking
of war with a gravity lost for a generation.
Not this year, they say, but in ten years perhaps,
twenty for certain. The politicians need it.
Europe again will be the terrain. It has
so much practice in being devastated.

I see the shape of the Shepherd on the wood's edge;
he emerges, hangdog, panting. The hare
has danced him to exhaustion
and escaped. I am as glad as if I
had heard the remission of Europe's fears.

Yet still I ask my mind how much longer
cuckoo will laugh to human ears his
message of delusion, and whether men will
learn in time the saving harmonies,
or poppy, cornflower and pimpernel
return to fields untilled.

On a Cat's Portrait

The Egyptian lapis cat
in the Louvre
shapes out divinity.
Goya's cat scowls
demoniac.

My cat, black-and-white
in art as in nature
thrusts the forepaw imperial
like the Shanghai British lion
whose mane is worn smooth
by the secretive palms
of luck-seeking proletarians.

Small-Hour Vigil

Small cat soul
hovering this night
on the verge of living
though not of being,
we keep the vigil
lying between sleep
and waking,
listening for those
cries that tear
us with your pain
and with reproach
for ease ungiven
and impossible.
It is not understanding
that ends, friendship
that vanishes. Our
eyes connect in
panic, knowing we all
have reached the
undelayable
period, your
seventh life
as I count it,
your first death.

What you seem to perceive
through eyes that grow
more crystalline
as you draw near
to darkness,
we know only — and perhaps
not at all — in
faith that all who live,
different, equal, of
many forms but of one
spirit are
compounded, hence
enduring.

Such lordly thought is
anodyne as your
cries demand the
comfort I am
for the first time unable
to provide, as I dread
the instant when
I must lift
and carry you
fragile and quivering,
in my hands to
the end of
life that was so
vivid and so
swift.

Lapwing

Head crested in black,
marked like a warrior's
helmeted head on a Greek
wine bowl, nature
parodying man, you
teeter on clods
and rise, broad wings
lapping as you soar
and bank, plaintively
calling Keewitz!
Peewit! — depending
on whether the hearer
is German or English —
as you dance me
away from the hollow
where your eggs like
a handful of earth
lie brown-speckled
and protected only
by the guile
of your
naive theatrics.

It is spring now,
with bird flocks fissured
to breeding pairs
but as I watch you
it is winter then,
and I a small boy
in a farmhouse window
under the Wrekin,
looking north over
ploughed Shropshire fields,
where lapwings wheel
and mass and
darken the horizon.

Day after day I stand
brow pressed on the cold panes,
mind spelled into longing
by that cry forlorn
so magnified, so distant
and so lost
that calls to lands,
unknown, unknowable.

The Disappearance

Late in the fall they came to our garden.
Varied thrushes; he bright in orange-banded
helmet, jet-black torque, she
duller, yet as hens go,
spectacular.

A month they rummaged,
kicking and tossing the brown leaves,
probing for grubs, calling in faded echoes.
The blue-eyed cat stalked, silent
and waited.

One day the hen had gone. All winter
the cock lingered, solitary and awkward
among juncos and chickadees,
jostling for the grain we scattered.

Three months pass. The start of April.
I look out early one morning; am happy.
Two orange flashes
under the pippin tree; the cock proud and
transformed, no longer bird Gulliver
among pygmies; the hen modest, and
industriously scrabbling for whatever
worms the spring has awakened.
Two days later they are gone
to nest in the safe forest.

Does the thrush mate
for a lifetime, I wonder?

The grey cat walks in the empty garden.

Species of Birds

I

Your summer self has left, migrating southward.
The darker species stays, hedge-furtive,
avoiding voices, leaving uneaten
the seed I spread in patterns on the snow.
I listen pointlessly. There is no song;
only a small hard click, less than a coot's,
and ventriloquial, seemingly not voiced
by that small shadow rustling in bare branches,
a winter bird whose presence is an absence.

II

And this bright raucous comer,
iridescent, blue, black-crested,
your screaming self of summer,
voracious, tumble-nested,
splendid, loud,
unabsent stridently
and proud
among brown hedge-creepers.

III

As birds both are,
so both are you,
from one self egg
in one strange instant
incubated.

Merlin I

Merlin
is the little hawk
that flies like a pigeon
and descending
on slanting wing
deceives small birds.
Do names merely
pun, or do
wizards
haunt the fence posts
waiting for the
magic night, the
golden dawn?

Merlin II

Merlin sits in his tree,
erect as a small eagle.
I walk through the beaten-down
winter hay, and he
rises, and I think
he is departing.
But he swings in
a narrowing spiral
that centres on my head.
He descends so close
that I see his eyes
like a tiny cat's
as his beaked mask turns
towards me, and the
flash of intelligence
is exchanged. He is only
ten feet above me
when the spiral breaks
and he flies away
over the vole tracks
in the derelict gardens.
Power departs.
A magic is
broken.

Arion Sings of His Rescue

I woke to hear them talking of my death.
Gold was the prize, my life the inconvenience.
One talked of knives. One of the axe.
One said a poet should have silken strangling.
The mildest spoke of drowning.
I ceased pretending sleep. The gold
was in their hands, guilt in their eyes
and anger in their voices. I did plead
not to be killed with blood. I asked
to suffer the sweet strangling of the sea.
I asked to sing one song before I died.
The mild agreed, the angry shouted,
yet as I strung my lyre fell silent,
and joined the others as the song was ending
to spill me in the sparkling waters.

No land in sight and archers on the deck,
I let my lyre float off and hopelessly
swam outward from the ship.
Then did the waters surge
with leaping bodies, and the dolphin's back
rose dark and glistening up between my legs,
and I rode singing on the summer sea,
and heard the dancing beasts around me sing
and, deep below, the ocean ringing
as the whales sang of the great freedom
in all their weight and wisdom, Leviathan
whose enemies were not yet born.

Then the cloud came, the sea grew wine-dark;
my song fell sombre for I saw the future,
Leviathan among his foes as I
among the robbing sailors, wisdom
losing its weight and weight its reason
as man, the cruellest of all
creatures and the most cunning,
destroys the great free beings of the earth.
I see the wild ass dead, the elephants stampede
towards extinction; in their death throes
trumpet the end of all whales' singing.

Does it console me as my song grows darker
that those who kill the free destroy
their own freedom, those who destroy
the wise die from their own folly?

I see an empty world, the whale's path
silent, and a lifeless waste
the elephant's ground, the cities sand and salt,
the last man drowning in the barren waters
and no beast there to answer to his song
and take him riding to the sands of life
where I wade in, embrace my brother beast,
and send him back towards the ringing depths.

Birthday Poem

For Marie Louise Berneri

March is that month, unstable as our life,
When, in last battle at the winter's edge,
Cold and the sun in fluctuating strife
Contest the year with stark, symbolic rage.
In that sharp fight is ever one sure end
When spring's heraldic colours win the land.

Let me then wish that, as the yellow days
Grow up in April from dark roots of winter
And life breaks out its green on haggard trees,
Your days may grow and bloom from this dark centre,
Golden and happy as the giving hand,
Unharmed by the unseasonal frost or knife-toothed wind.

Let me then wish that quiet flowers may shape
On all the spreading branches of your life
Opening the silent petals of friendship and the ripe
Fruit of love, protected by fortune's leaf,
That over your future the giant tree may grow
Rising from the meagre seed our efforts sow.

In fine, I give you the talisman of outward chance
Against the evil eye of luck and the bright
Finger of time. For you who have beauty for birthright
And grace in your heart, life can give no increase
Within yourself, but all external good
I would give you today if I had the touch of gold.

Deviation

You will find your way leaping like water
and misty past the rigour of resisters
flow, then rise beside the leaping water
verdant. A bending reed, but not a broken,
bows to the wind, erects towards the sun
till withering; yet while statues crack in frost,
are dust for ever, sends pale shoots again
and paler roots to shift the floors of forums,
until the bright eclipsing of all days
turns a soft answer on the teeth of death.

Ballad for W. H. Auden

As I walked out one evening,
    Walking down Granville Street,
The fog drained off the mountains
    And the air blew wet with sleet.

And there you walked beside me
    In the desert of my thought,
With your lost ambiguous brilliance
    And the wit time set at naught.

The glass was dark in your mirror.
    You held it. I looked in pain.
In that face turned lunar landscape
    I saw the earth of Spain.

I saw the arid valleys
    Where the quick and the dead still wait,
And I knew why your answer was silence
    And how silence shaped your fate.

I walked down Granville with Spender
    In a different, golden year,
And Spender said: "God and Auden,
    They call each other Dear!"

O master of my awakening
    Who made me hear aright,
O leader lost of my twenties
    Who elected for faith and flight,

O patient and private poet,
  Who blessed each hovering day
With prayer and vision and practice
  Both God-directed and lay,

And in the American desert
  Kept your Lent and your craft intact,
My mind makes me turn and salute you
  And life as an artifact.

But my eyes look in your mirror,
  I see the rived image it shows,
And my heart speaks out in answer
  And my desperation grows,

For what the glass has awakened
  Is neither envy nor joy
But the pity I felt at your passing
  In so narrow and wearing a way.

Yet your image speaks like a judgement
  As if your body declared,
"Let me accept the sentence
  And my brother soul be spared!"

If your Anglican God has received you
  As Auden or Wystan or Dear,
I know that all is accepted
  With irony, without fear,

As the fog drains off the mountains
  And the air blows wet with sleet,
Walking ghostly out one evening,
  Walking down Granville Street.

Elegy on Archers

For Philip Rigg

The archer stood, alone,
in the Indian cemetery
at Kitwancool, and unique.
No other Tsimshian carving
resembled that lithe
renaissance vision,
poised on his column,
the stringless bow
directed skyward
and the whole figure
bronzed with lichen,
made ethereal
by wood's decay.
Who carved him, and why,
in a village of solid
and sombre totems, nobody knew.
Long fallen, he has rotted
into the long grasses
by the sullen river,
yet loiters
in the dark of my memory
to return as your image,
sibling or double.

For you too practiced
that beautiful and archaic
art of accuracy
and destruction
and other arts of stark
and calligraphic beauty.
How far you understood
object and implication
of such hieratic modes
I never knew,
and yet you stand
in memory framed in them,
in figure like the vanished
archer of melting wood,
your bow sky-lifted,
your arrow drawn and driven
into the light
by which you lived
in which you die.

Mutational Blessing

For Margaret Atwood

Cased in their cool black gloves
those small fast hands,
by the opaque stone eyes
within masks directed,
can learn through swift
manipulative practice
most of the tricks of
pickpockets, latch-lifters,
and the evasions of
small Houdinis, yet,
thumbs unopposed, can
never bless. Raccoons
give through accepting
as the innocent
do always:
sanctify not.

Yet to be man-blessed
is in our age damning
to accidie or madness.
So I wish myself beast
at the crossing point of
thumb to bended pinkie,
the columned fingers
rising tripled between
innocence and knowledge
to the voice saying
pax vobis — and
nobiscum.

The Dream

For A. J. M. Smith

It all seemed very natural.
There was I, squatting
beside the border, dusty smell of
summer weeds on my hands, and you
stepping along the lawn, young
as I had not known you.

I thought you were mad, saying
you had come to see my river! You liked
that sort of thing, you said, pointing
over the lawn. It was then I wondered
if I were crazy. There it ran
cutting the lawn like a clear
new knife, a river
in miniature, glassy over
polished stones.
           I bent, dipped
my hand, licked the sweetness;
dipped again, lifted my cupped
palms towards you. You
were gone. I let the water
drip to the brown grass. The stream
flowed on.

On Jack Wise's Painting, "Igneous Rock"

Stone is for foundations
and for breaking.
At the moment
of creation
stone also
burns.

In the quaternary
wholeness of elements
that in all myth
and art is instinct,
stone in the purest sense
is fire and earth.

Stone relates also
to water,
gushing
in the desert,
and where the water
lies under
rocks, waiting
for divination,
and at Delphi enclosing
the spring of
Apollo, at Helicon
the Muses' fountain.

Stone is
safer than sand,
deeper — enclefted —
than doom, the
church's rock, the
scabbard of swords that give
title to magic
kingdoms, the
seat of kings, the
soul's refuge.

And though stone
by earth is pulled
defying air, yet
burns it fierily
when meteors drop
out of space where
stone lives weightless,
unattached, child
of the void,
where light
unburning
gleams.

In my mind's eye
I see, when it is absent,
your painting, rock
igneous, sign
of the burning
heart of earth,
and know the fires
that are it
and the air that
cools it
into solidity,
and the rains that
quench and shape it,
and there I see
symbols of our nature
enwholed, earth and
fire and
air and water,
nature's elements and
man's four humours
all in that omphalos
of lambent burning
combined and
reconciled,
at burning
peace.

On Seeing a Recent Photograph
Of Stephen Spender

A silver replica of golden youth,
the feminine, sensitive features —
mobile as glittering water
in recollection — frozen now
to austere maleness, he
looks through his own frame of
memory, the prophet facing
an unresponding future.

He is the silent
survivor of those voluble
mountaineers of the spirit,
frontiersmen from class
to class crossing,
and in the expected
Eden of virtues
proletarian, only mistrust
finding; the English
narodniki, gentlemen
with consciences and the
wrong accents.

All this was trying to
be more than poets, yet
the exaltation and the
disillusionment in finding
there was no glory or gratitude
earned for
revolutionary poses,
provoked their muses.
It was their words, not actions,
that glowed in the brightness
of desert
twilights.

Auden is gone and
Lewis and MacNeice,
by death dumbfounded.
Only this last old man
all passion desiccate
into the bones of thought,
survives from the last time
when poets saw like seers
and often saw aright.

Acrostic to Celebrate Resigning the Editorship of *Canadian Literature*

Going away is a kind of returning,
Entering again a mirror of oneself,
Or perhaps plunging into a sea cavern to
Recover what the years had hidden away.
Given that the task has been good, we all still
End with the longing for liberation.

Would I have started, I now ask, if
Others had not shown a mad confiding,
Or continued if my voice out of the unknown
Darkness had not roused others, an eventual
Chorus of critics? As Roethke would have it,
One learns from going where one has to go.
Criticism may be creation's left-handed
Kin, but is, too, offspring of the cruel muse.

Hell take such memories! Bell tolls, clock chatters,
And now's a time to march, like Flecker's pilgrims,
Never attaining the receding goal, perhaps, but
Daring what comes and yet not lacking
Sadness for all inevitably must end.

One says good bye to what one has been making, not in
Valediction, for it is mind out of one's mind,
Ever to be there like the departed child, but
Rendered free to receive a different

Turning, to accept a new guide and a new
Orchestration of themes, tunes and soundings.

Bill New in fact takes over; Woodcock goes.
If names have meaning, or if puns have point,
Let's have no doubt the future is renewal.
Let's also skip false modesty, self-deprecation.

No journal lived on hot air eighteen years.
Even so, urge declines as other urges rise, and
We (editorial form) depart, remain, and so say,
    (skipping beyond line, scansion, and acrostic
    form) : Le Rédacteur est parti! Vive le Rédacteur!

Souvenir of Menton

For Roy Daniells, 1902-1979

North from the seashore, in that meagre land
The olive trees give small and bitter fruit,
Yet in the cloven rocks, on branches stark and black
Persimmons burn like orange balls of fire
Taking into those groins of darkness the image of a sun
That on the winter seashore warms like love

And loads the lemon trees with their sharp-scented fruit.
Do you remember the Russian graves under the black
Cypresses shaped like flames, a sombre fire
Of memory, dark over the harbour where the sun
Has shone impartially on those who came for love
Or fled as fearful migrants from a violent land?

In the old town Saracen doorways opened on the black
Hearts of houses clambering the narrow streets as fire
Climbs upward. From those dark dens outward to the sun
Tall splendid girls emerged, adorned for love,
And even saints adored them in that land
Where gods were flesh and fish and even fruit.

Far in those hills the poems rose like fire
Out of the hearts of bards towards the sun,
And from the purlieus of the courts of love
The troubadours ran singing through the land
Those heresies of which the bitter fruit
Was war, Les Baux in ruins, and the black

Scourge of Montfort, the blinding of the sun,
The tongues torn out of those who spoke of love.
You and I knew this as we walked the land
Successive years and thought of history's fruit
And sought the flash of dewlight in the black
Ash of the past and dreamed that ash's fire.

You saw the dark as well, yet felt the love
Lost in the past of that bright used-up land,
Wrote exorcizing sonnets, ate the fruit.
A child stopped at a door sensing the black
Threat in a castle room. At Golfe San Juan the fire
Of empire faded, lost in its setting sun.

Past is that land. Your absence is now's fruit.
Yet in that black of loss the rising fire
Comes from your memory's sun, crescent with love.

Note to Octavio Paz

I remember you, Octavio:
a brisk winter's night
in Delhi, smell of
dungfires sharp in the
streets, Diwali lights
glittering from gold
and silk in a
rich Sirdarji's house:
we standing
by the white wall,
you saying: "How
delectable the
women, but
the men . . . !"

I have not seen you since
but remember you when
I look with
delight and gentle
lust at a friend's
wife's beauty, and
say: "How quickly
he is changing
for the worse!"

The Eye of the Phoenix

For Paul Huang

The eye is clear.

The eye of the phoenix
looks through fire
into water.

The water is only a surface
and the fire is beneath it.

The eye of the phoenix
is the fire
that consumes
creating.

The eye breathes out of ashes
and looks through its growing plumes
into the burning sky.

The Edge of Fire

For Ivan Eyre

Painting is language,
poetry is vision,
and from that inspired
confusion, that changing
of attributes, mating of
words with the wordless, of
form with intention, the
hills of our landscapes
emerge, under a sky
taut with time's tension,

never a sun
in that sky, but
brilliance, the splendid,
cosmic, benign.

Your hills give their soil
to a dark invasion. Their
forests, like others, are
made of trees, plantations
of pulpwood, reserves of
lumber, vulnerable to
falling and fortuitous
fire.

        The edge of fire
is the edge of vision
and these combustible
vistas, forests extending
to the edge of perceiving,
lead the eye into
the fire that never
destroys, the peace at
the edge of peril,
serenity emerging from
evil, eternity in Blake's
sandgrain, the ordering
that is peril and
power and the holy
weakness of those the
muse rides, of art's
proud submission.

Black Flag

Sand

In this air serene
Serfs who built the towers
Shall not live again
Or ghosts speak in the wires.

Yellow sand has drowned
Towers, parks and streets,
Flowered fecund ground,
Rocks with ammonites.

And from tawny soil
Geometric pines
Siphon turgid sap
Through ascetic veins.

But stark pines shall share
Fate of walls and spires
When the eroding wind
Sweeps these sandy shores.

And heroes who survive
The obsolescent wars
Shall rebuild the white
Streets and symbolic towers.

Steel Valley, 1938

War husks its rumours, and the yellow scurf
Of gorse scabs mountains over men who smote
Steel and trod surer feet on slag than turf.

But in their valley, where the fume clouds float
Only in memory and past-praising speech,
These men have learnt life to a meagre rote,

Achieve negation, but no wider reach
Span towards anger. Theirs the needy urge
That prompts the searching of the hungry leech

And tilts the sunning cups of dingy spurge,
Theirs the blunt memory of singeing blast
And prosperous creeping of the slag tip's verge.

Essentials only, cold and hunger, last.
Here stand no idols for the iconoclast.

The Silent Mills of Pentre

Behold the angina pectoris of an age!
The thousand metal replicas of the time's heart
slow already in bodies of brick and earth
until as pistons is the land's pulse still.

Thus is the start. Man's creatures dying first
crystal his end, and general stasis spreads
slowly, by town and land, by man and man.
Man dies. Only the men survive
to feel the insidious smothering of time
shut the world into an airless trap,
to fear the pangs that split their private breasts
presage the evening when the willing fuse
bursts the heart of the old from Pentre to Rome.

Landore

Fume-bitten no grassness of mountains,
barrenness not of summer,
meant the reek of copper rising up the valley,
seeping into houses, drying child lungs,
eating the heart of beauty
but keeping factories prosperous, bringing
dividends to shareholders, to the workers
bread in belly, freedom from absolute want, a little pleasure.

Now the dawn of grass sprouts, fire galvanic
bursts the yellow flowers, harsh green
new moss veins the stone brows,
birds nest on the mountain,
the air is pure and hunger is in the valley,
dereliction
of sag-roof factory and smokeless stack,
children suffering now the flaccid unfed belly,
young men squatting for talk in the lee of walls,
the slow round of mountain and stone-grey street,
pitch-and-toss on the slag heap,
walks by the scummed river,
The Red Flag sung like a dirge,
and the public library now and again of a morning.

The Valley

The bearded strangers who were glad to hear
Talk of islands and deserted mines
Had left the valley, driven by their fear.

Sun parched the fruit left on the blighted vines,
The eels were dying in the shrinking pools
And dead sheep festered in the empty lanes.

Signs were written on the cracking walls
In stubborn chalk — the prayers of men for rain,
Political curses and the japes of fools.

But from their homes the men who wrote had gone,
Gardens were grass, the mirrors yearned for faces
And trains stood empty on the splaying lines.

So future passing the deserted houses
Saw the tables spread, the food and half-full glasses.

Spring, 1939

Blunt hooks of vegetable gold
Lop the arthritic hands of cold;

Winter and the heraldic kings
Hasten on the bullet's wings.

But still the looker in the mirror
Sees Death grimace over his shoulder,

For Prague's March of blows and blood
Stains the bud in the English wood.

Cover your eyes. You cannot hide
Streets of England jammed with dead

Or fingers on the falling wall
Pointing the corpses on the hill.

The tocsin's whorls of brass are spun.
The slanting hands obscure the sun.

The Announcer's Speech

Forget the flowers like faces, seeds like skulls,
    The leaves like bayonets and bulbs like bombs,
Forget the ingenious noses hiding holes,
    The sharks' teeth fringing desiccated gums,
Forget devil and god, for this happy day
They walked out of town and went to stay.

You'll have happiness now, when no Groucho faces
    Tempt you to good or frighten to evil,
When no more orders from demons or angels
    Detail to die or, worse than dying, kill.
God skulks in Heaven, devil in Hell.
The rules are flyblown. No-one hears the bell.

You can grow roses now — there'll be no more blight.
    You can carry out plans for the lily pond.
You can write the interrupted five-act play.
    You can cease taking pills to make the heart strong.
You need never run again for the eight o'clock train
Now the Golden Age has fallen like backstage rain.

You are washed in the blood and clothed in the light,
    You are led by the lamb to the fields of joy,
Where you'll never meet want or work again,
    Bombs in the air or mines in the bay.
Death followed devil and god, this happy day
When they walked out of town and went to stay.

Sunday on Hampstead Heath

Underfoot on the hill the water spurts
Thickly out of the brilliant matted grasses
Where the slopes fold in groins and thighs of earth
And the winter sunlight in thin golden masses
Falls through the lungeing wind that swings the skirts
Of the girls walking with their soldiers over the Heath.

A group of dwarf fir trees marks the crest
With boughs like drowner's hands that claw the sky.
Far down the slope a white springboard rears
Its gaunt and skeleton frame above the grey
Tossed pool where in summer the boys raced
But where now only the ducks bob, resting their oars.

Leaning their weight on London, the smoky roofs
Below the hill stretch out their infinite folds,
A stony sea, far in miasmic depth
Where men sleep out their empty dreams of deeds,
And towers and domes, surging like green reefs,
Rise up heroic and powerful in their sloth.

Here on the hilltop my friends and I sit down.
They talk of prisons; the conversation falls
And I say: "One evening we must drink at the Spaniards."
I do not know what they are thinking as their heels
Kick out the turf and their gaze creeps over the scene,
Peering through the smoke for the customary landmarks.

But, going away in my mind from their shut faces,
Away from the quiet hilltop and the leisurely men
Digging in their new gardens below in the little valley,
I enter the forest of rooftops; under the grimy stone
I walk among the pipedreams of men in braces
Reading in Sunday newspapers the end of faith and folly.

And in the broken slums see the benign lay down
Their useless empty loves, and the stunted creep
Ungainly and ugly, towards a world more great
Than the moneyed hopes of masters can ever shape.
In the dead, grey streets I hear the women complain
And their voices are sparks to burn the myth of the state.

And here where my friends talk, and the green leaves spurt
Quietly from waterlogged earth, and the dry leaves bud,
I see a world may rise as golden as Blake
Knew in his winged dreams, and the leaves of good
Burst out on branches dead from winter's hurt.
Then the lame may rise and the silent voices speak.

Poem for Michael Bakunin

The wayfaring tree walks heavy for the winter,
The multifaceted eyes of evenings
Lean down into their darkness
Like lights on sinking ships
And the whistling ghosts follow us in the streets.

The black and white of gravestones under the lash
Of flowing branches hurling bobs of life
Seeds in the mind the morrows feared and far
That soon will join their tips
Into a day more burning than the sun.

For that dry future, when these tiny flames
Grow into one to burn both fear and hope
And when life's day spills on a ruined land
The iron growth of stars where green guns grew,
Shall be more violent than our eyes can hold.

And in that instant, when time's two worlds meet
And day's destructive urge breaks down the dark
To set a furnace in a dying age,
Our little selfish loves and days shall wane
Beneath a glowing and perptual noon.

Elegy for Emma Goldman

For those who, magnolia tall, confront us,
Stately and pale, gods of a golden earth,
And south's inheritors of suns and status,
There is no place among the quiet shadows
Of grey men drenched in brine and crowned with dirt,
There is no kingdom in the drowning furrows,
Or under the brimming towers, ambiguous trees
Where the dead water and women find their peace.

Sad are cities where freedom stings like cancer;
Not for the fortunate their eyeless evenings
Where tears are stagnant and death stands as a fencer
With the ready point of doom above the helpless.
Here those in silver gendered and sired by kings
Are blind to the dark stigmata on rotting faces,
And their happy superior days end without meaning
In iron forests where only the drunken sing.

The trees starting in semaphores from my earth
Signal a life more simple and more wise
Than those who were happy, without thought, from birth.
So you, Black Emma, walking the evil streets
With horror etched as a map upon your eyes
And the blood of anger rising in trees from your breasts
Carried a need as single in your heart
As the sap rising in the Spring's young heat.

Kinetic as a plant the purpose rose
High from your head among the sterile stones
Of many million people and no hopes.
Not for the feckless were the flowers you bore,
Not for the dying waiting for dead men's bones,
Not for the visages consumed by fear.
Only for the evil cities and the grey, trodden men,
For the poets and drowning women your black blooms shone.

An age bursting like a well at winter's depth
Spills on the cities its sad and brutal night.
The day we are born to is ebbing from the earth,
The day that gave our comfort and their need
And the common living death in the hard sunlight
Where beauty wilted in the noon of greed.
The evening ends. We cannot see what day
Lies past the night we enter under an evil sky.

But in that day those tongues we shall remember
That spoke, in the dead years, of pride and freedom;
We shall remember their goodness and their anger.
Our minds will hear them from the quiet grave;
Their dreams will shape the margins of our futures
Till mental cords shall drop from every slave.
Then you will walk the daylight of our thought.
Now our deeds remember you in the night.

Tree Felling

The bright axe breaks the silence in the wood.
The ivory chips spray over crushed nettles,
And the red slender pine sways and totters
Shuddering its boughs in the chill of death.

All down the hill the yellow teeth of stumps
Stud the tramped moss and broken willow herb;
The piled long boles point northward to the Pole,
Their fragrant lymph seeping from broken veins.

And borne away in the blue wake of tractors,
The lopped trees leave for ever their fitting landscape;
Soon they will grow again in the underground valleys
Where the naked miners crawl under a sagging sky.

And here the ploughs will traverse, as in Carthage
Marking the end of a kingdom, the day of the squirrel
And the blue jay chattering along the mossed alleys
Between the still pines. The silence of felted needles,

Spawning in ugly toadstools and sick brown orchids,
Has ended that seemed unending. Cyclic transition
Will reign on the hillside, with bare and ice-baked winter
And multitudinous summers under the whispering corn.

The Little Trees

The little trees, steepening up the hill,
With empty basins spread beneath their boughs,
Show the contour of the vanished wall.

Each spring the dwindling veterans planted roses
And paper cornflowers by the upgrown road.
Now, only the agaric grows,

For the veterans are dead or old
In the valley where the young once more
Toil day and night,
With iron, blood and gold
To build again the falling wall of fear.

Poem for Garcia Lorca

Count on dead fingers of time the years that pass
Since Lorca sang his last of Spain
And fell beneath the hard inhuman paw,
Gasping between white walls in Granada.

Lorca, the song of men whose emptying hearts
Sang out the seconds of their death in blood,
The song of women whose bloodless futures lay
Twisted under the roof of tyranny.

Remember Lorca as Spain's noblest bull,
Not in the sunlight of Mithraic rings
Spurting his life to matadors and crowds
But in numb secrecy to the knacker's laugh.

Remember Lorca as the earth of Spain,
Lined with valleys as an old man's hand,
In each valley the gun lurking and the dead waiting
For the dawn that will not break their empty sleep.

Remember Lorca as the poor of Spain,
Rising once from their alleys of quiet death
To wash with blood the roots of barren trees
That do not bloom this year and one year will fall for ever.

Remember Lorca, who died only for being Lorca.

On Completing a Life of Dumont

A year I have lived the most of my mind with you,
Acting your deeds as best I can, thinking your thoughts, and
Now I stand back, take your dark presence in my view,
And realize that though we say goodbye, easy hand
In hand, like companions ending a long hard journey,
We are still strangers, you from your world where
Violence is what happens in the natural daily way
Between animals and between man, I from the rare
Interlude of a time where peace has been a fragile
Possibility in a few favoured places for a few.
But what is the echo I hear compellingly ring
In my ear as you bow sardonically into your defile
Of dark death? What does it tell me I share with you?
Is it, fierce stranger, that freedom is a word our hearts both sing?

Paper Anarchist Addresses the Shade
of Nancy Ling Perry

Out of our daylight into death you burn,
    For words once lit you, sparks struck out of books,
And as you char to memory I learn
    How words life-tempered bend to cruel hooks.

Among those words perhaps some were my own,
    Written within the fiery coil of youth,
When ambiguity was left unknown
    And consequences seemed no bar to truth.

Truth as then seen, sharp white and shadow black,
    And as you saw it, leading through flame's dawn,
        The only causes time and fear and place
Why you, not I, enter that violent dark
    And I look on, appalled, ashamed, and mourn
        Terrible children, comrades, enemies.

Black Flag

When I die
let black rag fly
raven falling
from the sky.

Let black flag lie
on bones and skin
that long last night
as I enter in.

For out of black
soul's night have stirred
dawn's cold gleam,
morning's singing bird.

Let black day die,
let black flag fall,
let black rag fly,
let raven call,
let new day dawn
of black reborn.

Black Rose

For M.L.B.

This is the black
rose of memory.
It has taken
a long time
to spring from
the briar of
silence.

Ago twenty-seven years,
away half a world,
you gasped for breath
and died
while I voyaged
to a new land:
by your death severed,
a new life.

On bleak Atlantic,
April off Halifax,
I dreamed your death
and scoffed at the dreaming.
Could youth and such
beauty
be doused like
a candle?
The cable awaited.
You were dead.

What could I say,
heart clogged with grief,
the muse departed?
Despair is
inarticulate.

I had written you love poems;
I could not write
your elegy,
or make bloom again
the rose uprooted.
My grief found
no image
to speak through
and I became
a silent poet.

The silence is ended.
Sorrow in its long
subterranean working
has made its own roots,
its own briar,
its own thorns,
its own rose;
which is the black
rose of memory
that I offer.

Its colour
will never offend
an anarchist shade,
and in its dark heart
you live in your
brightness and beauty
that age never
withered,
while I serve
your memory
in the antique temple
of a crumbling
body.

To Marie Louise Berneri,
Twenty-eight Years Dead

Now I am old,
false-toothed and almost bald
and ruby-nosed from drink,
all but my mind decayed,
and even my mind, no doubt,
clogged up with care and caution.

And you have been dead
almost as long as you lived —
those thirty years of beauty
and incandescent spirit
lost in three decades of absence.

You never did grow old,
you never lost your looks
or felt your mind
lapse out of confidence.
The cause was always unsullied,
our triumph was always assured;
Bakunin had laid the word down;
Kropotkin has proved it by science.

I dreamed of your distant death
the very hour it happened.
You came in another dream
to complain in solitude
in strange whine like the dead
crowding around Odysseus.

Since then other women
populate my dreams
with their temptations
and denials. You,
whom I loved and grieved
like a self, never appear.

Yet it is as if
you were always there
on the edge of consciousness,
your ideas echoing
in what I wrote, my thought
still touching yours.

And sometimes when the mind
waking slips out of gear
and out of time, those years
when we worked together,
mind tuning into mind,
seem never ended. The eye
of memory is open
and the vision it denies
when I strive for recollection
is there without willing
and you are as you were
your own short life ago,
laughing within my mind,
prophecying Utopia
within your lifetime, and
filling the hearts of
those who watched you with
rage and sweetness.

Utopia has arrived.
You would not recognize
or like it. We are still
hoping for liberation
but do not expect it.

I have been as free as
any man, have succeeded
in all my personal aims,
and yet I have failed
what we both strove for.

Perhaps it was the impossible
and you could have achieved
no more. But you were spared
both failure and success,
their varying corruptions,
and you move in the mind's eye
untouched by the knife of age,
spared by the cancer of doubt.

You are a shade
                    and I am flesh
yet which of us
                    has died?

A World at War

Les Baux – August 1939

Day melts as deities of snow.
No more the hand against the sun
Shows the deathless parallels
In glowing signatures of bone.

And to American and old
Youth returns with rising dead,
Whose intimate spectres wake a world
Unseen under the night's head.

But deadlier resurrections haunt
Me and other landless young.
The precipice weeping like a girl,
The fever calling like a wrong.

And love who ruled the blinding walls
Sinks a corpse across our night.
Not Berengaria, but the guns
Stand lean backs against the light.

So eyes are glazed in the dying houses,
Silenced the lycanthropic song,
Where, over the cooling faces,
Sleeps the spread, incredible wing.

Fall, 1939

For Julian Symons

The thunder warning cracks. Our day is spilt
Into the glitter of the little bays
That lift the vivid prows of drifting craft
Towards the mimic islands of the haze.

Bound for a tamarisked and temperate shore
The boats have left without us. We remain
Like the cut-off explorers on the ice,
To face the winter, dearth and iron rain.

Such season resolute as they never thought
Our hearts must be to show rejected white.
Caught in a violent hour we did not want
We must endure till this time's ice-floes split,

And to such bays the boats put in again,
Bearing the letters from a land thought lost,
The cakes in tins and photographs of friends
To please a spring that flowers like the past.

Christmas Sonnet, 1939

For Lily Gold

From this sad planet, where the tragic are
Set in their tears like silence, I regard
Black space and every far and frigid star,
Whose brightest fire in distance shines like cold,
And know in envy white's celestial spray
That spreads as drops each bloodless, manless world.

Once stars as angels sang to this dark day,
When planets signed the quick essential man,
But blood and clay submerge the high and free
And no worlds sign or sign, but burn again
Millenial fire or cool to styptic ash
Unbitten by the dirty tread of men.
What gaseous gods there live, what fleshless flesh,
Earth's lord is lovely only in his wish.

Troy

London is near, but even the air
Bears no noise to this quiet field
Where shawled women creep the dark furrows,
From bagged aprons dripping potato seed.

This month shadows of the elm are green
And hang like creepers on the standing cart.
Spring makes solid with new leaves the hedge
That walls the stillness like an earthen fort.

Past the living ramparts of this Troy
Enemies lie but cannot kill its peace,
Where, denying the sieging force of time,
Moves monumental labour of the race.

But there will be a day when hedges part,
Admitting the plausible effigy, whose womb
Drops angry peril to crush the fertile plants
And exile peace to a far home.

Poem In April 1940

The slick adultery, the facile rhyme,
All quaint experiments die out on time,
Now death's a greedy god in every home.

For now the calendar and clock dictate
An iron limit and a measured fate,
The bursting heart, the cry, the slinking feet,

And through the window where my hope burns out
Cracks in the gun and time's recruiting shout;
The luckless instant when the glasses split,

Or lucky second when a coward half
Marries a strong, arboreal in the self
Rigid against a world too dead to save.

Battle of Britain

A fakir's rope of smoke hooked in the sky
    Marks the copse that shags the facing hill,
The burnt angles tangling the trees in steel
    And the banks of cyclists building a motley wall.

A stumbling cortege reaches the chilly sun
    Trampling a slow path through the kneeing grain.
The bundle in their arms is the aviator,
    Shrouded in coats his locked face of pain.

He was young. He will burn again
    Vicariously in dreams. The smoke thins into blue.
Cyclists return to their tandems. On the heath
    Swivel and roar the yapping snouts of guns.

Pacifists

The icy, empty dawn cracks in the fields
Under our labouring feet. We cross the fallow
With billhooks on our shoulders sloped like guns,
Drawing dark lines in rime white as we go.

Standing in filthy ditches in leaking boots,
We fell the towering hedges like Jericho walls
Under the blast of day. Around our feet
The water seeps and numbs through invisible holes.

Strange we have come, from library and office.
Hands that have never toiled, myopic eyes
And sloping backs revolt in an alien time.
Under a dead sky we expiate our oddness.

Having left friends and substitutes for love
In the leaning fragments of a distant city
We tread the furrows of infertile fields
And rediscover our pasts in a wet country.

Under our ineffectual misery, our boredom
And the empty sequence of unprivate days,
The lost squalors of the city become our end.
The cause that brought us dwindles. We hate blank skies,

Biting wind and the black bones of trees,
The promise of spring as a green omen of toil.
We rest our billhooks and talk of a starlit town
As the weak sun breaks on the land without a hill.

Wartime Evening in Cambridge

Silhouette of elms against an eggshell evening.
The green Cam slithers beneath me, the yellow girl
Rubs my shoulder, and the uniforms in blue
Direct their dummies to the ultimate kill.

Worn corners of cloisters, walls and turrets
Supporting space. The inexplicable voids of age.
But heavy feet are fettered; under the gateways
Shadows shining like iron maintain their siege.

Skies snow black rooks upon the leafless trees.
The jackdaws rustle to sleep on studious houses.
Mass-souled, the starlings throb towards the fen,
To the night that brings more deadly wings than theirs.

What Marxian spectre lays its beard on the evening?
What twilight have we committed? What blank sin
Broken upon the earth to rage for pardon?
What blood drips what inexpliable stain?

The boys that are marked to die, and the mad women
Driving their lovers to death for a cheap song,
And the men who will be leaded names on gravestones;
Passing, these cannot solve the brooding evening's wrong.

And watching the fading colours, the dimmed horizon,
The white faces becoming vague under the shadow,
I see an age that will not end for many
Draw its own death like a blind across a window.

Behind Trinity

Behind Trinity the liquid green slides down
Under Venetian bridges, lapping the solid green
Of old lawns funnelled by golden crocus, swept
By the long, fingery brooms of willow boughs.
This moment the mask of an evil time has slipped.
It is the orders and the tramping feet are false.

It is an illusory evil present that passes
As falling beauty breaks the reflected faces
That gibber from pools and mirrors the speech of death.
Here and for the instant I am eternal,
Swept out of time as dustmotes swept in breath,
Until the hours ring and here and present fall.

The Conshy's Lament

Rain slashes the brown clods of my acre,
Breaking tilth for the seed and avid roots.
I sit in the gloomy doorway of my shed,
Lighting my pipe and taking off my boots,

And think of yesterday's blue and the shouting planes
Courting like kestrel over my digging back,
Dancing to death down the roaring air,
Screaming through cirrus above eye's peak.

So in this gloom my heart a seed of sorrow
Grows towards graves and through the gaping skull.
My hands can feed the plant and feed the children;
They cannot sustain the dead against death's will.

Through veils of rain the stranger at the gate
Waits invisibly, but will not be late,
While the wet wind wails its descant of hate:
"The kind and the killer shall share one fate."

The Ruins of London

Those hurrying taxis, lovers fingering thighs
Towards the termini of journeys and desires,
Pass with fixed stares of round, inanimate eyes,
Irrelevant this evening as the dying saurian;
And old men homing, senile and unfair,
Tramp the cold avenues of cruel stone.
Only the unformed young and the formless old
Wear now the fabulous stones of gainless gold.

In the mock arson of the falling sun
The girls, lovely and ugly, tap their heels
Escaping in subways from the stinging rain
And the hour's fear of the returning bomber.
For these, the youths, the dotards and the girls,
Dinners are waiting and the cinema
Prepares a drug — more sinister than god —
To render hearts as docile as the dead.

For this is the city where death had dominion,
Whose mansions were the grandiose tombs of youth,
Grey catacombs where freedoms slept in line,
Poisoned by gold or strangled by the law,
Granite sarcophagi of love and truth
Where the divine lay slain and stuffed with straw.
Death wore disguise before. We did not miss
Our unlived lives or feel his quiet kiss.

City most lovely at twilight or the dawn,
When the blind grope like toads and the mad
Limp like devils, when the poor and fearful spawn
Under the earth, anticipating graves,
City, when your red evening on my head
Falls like a breath, like desiccated leaves,
How shall I view the wounds upon your walls,
Your bloody minarets and disembowelled halls?

Ignoring the lecherous idylls of the old
And colourful predilections of the rich and time,
I walk the dusty pavements drenched with blood
And scarred with flame twice in a city's life.
I see the archways built on sweat and crime
Breaking over the knees of Europe's strife
And Wren's white splintered pediments remain
Above the altars prayers could not sustain.

The public hands of frozen clocks declare
Perpetual and apocalyptic instants
Of crashing walls and towers flung through air.
The supple planes that bent before the blast
Are green above the fallen monuments,
The metal gods of privilege and caste
Whose eloquent tongues could not foretell the ends
Death's cunning wrought through their own fleshless hands.

The glassless windows hang like birds in trees.
The avalanches of stone balance as boxers
For the careless tread under the hanging eaves.
The rusty girders twist themselves like worms
Above that dry debris of safes and ledgers
Spread under dust in gold's deserted rooms
Where the typist's mirror hangs upon its nail
Reflecting boughs that bud where towers fall.

Lovely at last in sorrow the city stands
Niobe over her dead. What memories burn
Through time towards this hour, towards these ends
Where words become Phoenix, where our deeds congeal
In rock like ancient footprints, cannot turn
The dying pitiful past upon its heel.
The wounds of change transmute both man and race
As iron erodes the city's stony face.

Shall we open our veins and die like Romans
Sinking under despair in sleepy crimson baths?
Shall we project our journeys to new lands,
Seeking our hope beyond the far and future?
Shall we sit in towers and ponder abstract truths
While men bat-shouldered, cloaked and sinister
Prepare their childish and irrelevant schemes
To kill the priests and poison all the streams?

Death's tocsin rings the blood! What bodies fall
Under this rubble cannot rise to love!
Though we may build our future towers tall
To tip the sky like Babel, time will grant
No despite in decaying, age will leave
No man immune from the attentive ant.
Caught in death's gambit all our struggles end;
Cities and men checked by the same sure hand.

Wartime Poem from London

For Hugh Ross Williamson

The fading whistles outline our broken city
Against the dead chart and distant zodiac,
Against the decaying roads, empty and perilous
That join our exile with the land we seek.

Kissed onward by the pistol, we are all exile,
Expatriate, wandering in the elusive streets
Of faked identity, which swing towards a past
That is no Indies regained by circuitous sea routes.

The bridges are down, the visas are invalid;
We cannot turn on our tracks away from fate.
I stand at the phone and listen in to death,
And dare not stuff my ears and ring off hate.

Yet I behold an angel like a falcon
Bearing a speaking flame across the dark
To sing in the dumb streets of cretin-children
For the silly hearts that cannot even break.

And under the windows of a drunken pub
A man sits, listening, like a wind-squat tree,
Unnamed, his face a map of paper, his bone hands
Moulding from the burning voice a phoenix day.

Waterloo Bridge

The arms flicker like signals in the sun,
The rhythmic oars flash silver up the stream,
And through the green and stormy lakes of plane
Glide the black angels and the ghosts of peace.
On Waterloo Bridge I am thinking of a name
Written in lead, I am thinking of ashes,
I am thinking of graveyards billowed like a lake,
I am thinking of death's searchlights that will flower the dark.

And again, I am thinking of the angels and William Blake.
I imagine Blake in his chariot over St. Paul's,
And Swinburne fast as a plane above the Park,
Homing from spurious sin to smugness at the Pines.
Donne in his shroud is descending on Sadler's Wells
And through this peopled air pulse spectral tunes,
The infant Mozart and decrepit Handel
Competing in the wind's orgasmic rise and fall.

These spectres say our errors are returning,
Snake-eyed, to bury us. They say only our hells
Are repetitive, and in vain we long
For the rebirth of momentary heavens.
In the symbolic silence of the bells
As the hour strikes, softly they lean and warn
Against our hopes, our loves, our petty goods,
Then float to higher heavens, balloons and gods.

This is the preposterous hour when Caesars rise,
Bleeding, from their beds in the burning sea.
The dead are cashing in on all our follies.
They are not men and women, they are not divine,
These spirits bred of our own villainy.
It is ourselves who gibber at the pane,
Clanking across our age magnetic fetters,
Skywriting madness in incandescant letters.

This evening aviators crumple on killing earth,
This evening Trotsky is dying. Blood for blood
Seeping from birth and cataclysmic death
Mars the pale sky where gulls and flags are flying,
And love is failing where but hate is good.
This evening, I perceive, we are all dying,
We are all dying, like Wilde, beyond our means,
Dying, as sheep, for our folly rather than sins.

A malady like a journey is killing us slowly.
On the long inconstant travels of the mind
Towards the paradise we are approaching daily
But never reach, on endless days in the sun
Walking the deserts of our insular land
Between the pectoral hills and the salt lagoon,
We are haunted each evening by time's gorgon face;
The sickness of change is rotting our lives like ice.

I make the image of death, symbolical god
With spear and book, the angel of every aspect,
The joking fisher, devil with vulpine head
And mutable image of deity and man.
I imagine also the impersonal fact
Knitting the end of a maturing plan
And insubstantial force whose iron need
Draws down to earth the flower sapped with seed.

I imagine the frozen gesture of the loved
Made in the silent room, the rigid hand
Rising to the crying mouth and bowed head
Solid and grey as stone. The fearful lives of the lonely
Fail in an emptiness that is an end
More for the left. To those who have lived only
In their own hearts death must always be near
Among evil quiet and the steady voices of fear.

I see the plane caught in crossed hands of light,
Lurched in white spits of fire, till sudden flame
Splits in the sky, an instant hell of fate
Tearing the flesh and metal, mind and life
Into atomic agony and dusty doom.
I see the grasping hand above the wave,
The face in the fiery window, the ragged cross
Of the climber spread beneath the precipice.

But these are not the death in all the faces.
Not the stiff slain, but we the living die
Daily among the city's beautiful houses
And mortal streets, under the knowing speech
Of clocks and the togaed gestures of the high
Snatching with metal hands a world beyond our reach.
Time is our death. Our death is also life.
We are slain by what it is a death to leave.

For us, my love, there is no peculiar escape.
The pass is kept and frontiers of the mind
Barred by the unseen we cannot overleap.
I on this bridge, you in the speeding train
Framed in the window in your farewell stand,
Travel the one evil journey of the brain
For the perennial peak. As others striving
We share in their insidious death of living.

For us the sound of history is growing faint,
For us the distances are opening and now is as soon
Past as it is beginning. On this tremulous point
Crowded like angels in the schoolman's mind
We hang in sufference of the hastening sun,
We hang in sufferance of the sweeping hand.
There are no far lands for us, as we await,
Already dead, death to confirm our fate.

This is an autumn whose leaves are falling iron
Shed by a deciduous sky upon our hope.
The metal leaves are blotting out the sun,
The falling sky is crushing out all love
In this sad land wherein our futures weep.
In this dry land our weeping cannot save
Only the stone heart is immune from pain,
Only the automaton outlives the steel rain.

So we are dead who could not make in life
That peace in beauty which our gods ordained,
So we are dead beneath the withered leaf
Of worlds aborted by our winter's stroke,
Our thin delusions by now's evening stained.
Cursed by a present that in weakness broke
In blood and dust, we also were too weak
To shun the common nemesis of the sick.

Yet I recall the evenings marked in time,
The whispered intimations and the vague fingers
Of youth, when landscapes, as my thoughts, were calm
And when the dusky mirages of heaven
Cloaked in their mist the bloody teeth of dangers,
And the evil eye that orders odd or even.
Time was the voices speaking from the wood,
Fiery chariots rising through the splitting cloud.

And from the bridge, above the windy planes,
The flickering signals and the grey river,
Above the girls, above the silvery vanes
Pointing the winds set for homeric wests,
Above now, above this pointed here,
I see the statues rising from their rests,
The famous riding again above the city
That dies beneath their iron galaxy.

These are the praised, remembered in verse and stone,
Multiplied in the actions of the living,
These are the great whose earthly death has grown
In an existence greater than their death.
Above the striving and above the raving
They soar, as vast as gods, as light as breath.
I know they did not fail, they did not die
As we who live our dying blasphemy.

I know no world infected their desires
Or sapped their deeds. Lapped into their own souls,
Strong within strong, coiling their moving fires
In metal fires, in spiritual rock,
From an involvulate power of their wills
They sprang above the flesh, the chance and luck
Of daily evils undermining love,
And the deepening lesser deaths we live.

So they defeat the double death of man,
Our present death and death that makes an end
Of blood and monument. The lantern brain
Lit them a way I see that we must run
If we, my love, would live beyond the hand
That coils our life into a twist of pain.
Our selves within our hearts we must create
Like seeds in flowers and flowers involvulate.

We who are dying, like phoenix on the flame
Must burn our now and re-enact each self
Out of the agony of expiring same.
We must erect, within the circled soul
A centre warm to our peculiar life,
Signed by our individual breath and will.
We, as the rose, must blossom at the heart,
Closed like the flesh sea flower against death's hurt.

Then, as the growing music of the deaf
Erects its heaven within the closing skull,
May we achieve the harmonies that live
Beyond our little death, re-edify
The subtle architecture of the will,
Live above life, who die and daily die;
In the blank chaos of the faltering hour
Make of our blood the Babylonian hour.

Inside Vienna, as the cannon spat
Mortal destruction on the breaking walls,
Death on the child's brick halls, Beethoven sat
With ears unhearing but within the mind
Music unbroken heard. The interlacing hells
In and without the city were unkind,
But in the room, the chamber of his brain,
Music outgrew the immanance of pain.

Here is the map and symbol of our way.
Not a man lives who has not, under fire
Of steel or love, felt the desire to die
As we who die, the millions sham alive.
But music in the spiritual ear
Ignores the deadly world and thus, my love,
Breathing, as gods, our mountain air of truth,
We may escape the daily hour of death.

On Waterloo Bridge I am thinking of a name
Written in fire. Yet fires end in ash
And here I wonder if our hopes are dream,
If voices whispering in the evening river
Speak in my ear the prophecies I wish,
If still for us death is the only saviour
From the mean lesser deaths our failures make
Under the deadly flowering of the dark.

Eros and Thanatos

Stony Beach

You, and the stony beach
crushing into our flesh
its nodules hard from hate

the stony beach and the fall
of waves on the nether sand

and you on the stony beach
your eyes veiled with grey lids
your hair a pattern on stones

I bruise you with my hands
your laughter hits like stones

Now

Now I compare the forecasts with events,
Noting the lucky prophecy of each seer,
It is no calm of courage in the spring
That has out-driven my autumn fear.

It is no certainty of hiding safe
From steel or the conscripting hand of death
Swells my eternity like a tube of peace
Lipped to the wet staunchness of the earth.

Only the pattern of your wishing parts
Me so from fate. I cannot be afraid,
Though unheroic, when the nightmare gods
Pass dangerously as sniping flight of lead.

You are invisible friendship in this forest,
Warning the shadows and the bladder ogres;
You are the solid hand driving from highways
Talking ghosts and cannibal women-fakers.

You, speaking and silent with me, and loved
Here and away, make Now a lucky land
Where the electric walls bar fear's black hour
And many flowers turn gold from the happy hand.

But Now, authentic Phoenix, dies as lives.
Now lasts only as instant. Now is land
Where the events are, Now is not event,
And when the events attack, what walls shall stand?

Insular Poem

Cast on your beaches, whose flexed currents throw
Men and thoughts as brash, I rise and view
Your island face, whose tides without moon
Make palms mirage and valleys without sun.

Those like Gerbault who escaped by sails
Or sought the unknown Alpine above hills
Leave I lonely distance when I dare
Black and thicket jungle of your hair.

And drawn by soil magnetic of your mouth,
As sailors going native in the south
Burn their clothes and photographs of home,
I let tides gulf all craft wherewith I came.

Till, exile and expatriate for you,
Cut off from past by love's marooning flow,
I am Selkirk standing on the only island
Or last man on the last submerging strand.

Winter Sports

Gone in September, gone to friendlier climes
    Of azure cloudless skies and yellow sands,
Now flaunt you here to fascinate fond eyes
    No crimson-taloned horror of dead hands.

Now know numb lips no call of glistening lips
    Raddled to riper petals of desire;
Now know cold eyes no shrivelling fire of eyes
    Lit in hot holocausts of tropic fire.

Now limber lithe and swaying sleekly torse
    Now drowsy droop of full and fragrant breast
Ripen no anger of unwilling loins.
    Lust's climacteric eases in heart's rest.

But years swing cyclic, Spring from winter rising,
    And you who went with migrant swifts departing
Shall light your arson in cold hearts again.
    From death there is no parting.

Time

Now the silk ladder of impeccable hours
Turns to a noose for the unwary foot,
For love is lightning cindered, and our youth
Spattered to leaves of blood on our own walls,
Till, quick death past, the spreading rot of age
Bloats all beauty, petrifies all eyes,
When in the hothouse wilts the arctic wonder
And castled cards fall in the crack of thunder.

Yet as the ephemeral singer does not die
Till records crack, you shall survive your skin,
Your voice shall speak from all the telephones,
Your form shall rise from shaping of all stones,
Your steps shall follow me in all the lanes.

White

White is the evening nature of my thought
When neutral time that drains the night of green
Flows through the dusk in mimic dawn of white.

So pale the distance where blue morning shone
Knits in the whitest crises of our stars,
Burning the nightly ambience of alone,

And evil evident of coloured hours
Dies in this dark, whose sexless shapes of black
Are only active in our twilight fears.

For at day's death the whitest needs awake
When seeping pallor undermines the night
And white submerges all in evening lake,

Where, as a lode attracting all time's light,
You are white's evening nature of my thought.

Colours

In this emaciate form that is no shape
And symbolled is by change, the lines erect
No constant image on the shifting scape.

Nor, as the colours burn and interact,
Can they be fixed each in perpetual shade
But all must age, as mutable as fact.

Thus, in the dull of cold, fire's reds must fade,
Spring's greens and goldens drab in August drought,
Skies wane in night's anaemia of lead.

So, where all colours join, symbolic white
Grows dark with time and dirties in the sun
Shedding all brilliance in dusk's death of light.

And you, in whom white's beauty once was stone
Discard all light in time's corroding stain.

Silent Distance

Now the dreams are over and sunbeams stand
Vertical spectres over your far head,
Fear approaching in a slanted hand
Severs my morning as a sudden blade,
And I am dark where silence is a night.
Whiter though day than ice, I dare not see
What distance opens like a gulf in light,
Parting by more than breadth your thought and me.

Miles are a measure of no heart or thought
But loved are distant when their silence hangs
Dark as a fog between the sun and sight.
So fear expands like water's stone-born rings
As cloud advances on my morning's white,
Stifling in silence noon's Babylonian tongues.

Arles

Aigues Mortes

Earth is the town that squares my eye
And out of salt the strength of bone
Builds the citadel high and high
Over the gardens growing stone.

Into stone the faces grow.
The pectoral contours set in rock.
Heat burns the heart as dead as snow
And beauty sleeps like shells in chalk.

Salt on the eyelid and the lip
Tortures the flesh too tired for tears.
The visions into marshes slip,
Sink and are lost beneath their fears,
And in such land of mire and stone
Your absence withers all my green.

Hour and Place

This is the break of fire flaunt, stubborn life,
And is the pyrotechnic stair of change
Where self so sunder so asplinter set
Swells in love's spume dash and night's clap of wave
Towards the man whose hour and place are heat.

Behind the fuschia barriers of the heart,
Within the trim white houses of the brain
The omens like homunculi increase
That enemies are in the belly's fort
And times converge upon the fruit of years.

For is the north wind blowing in the breast,
Is thunder gathering in the burning reins
To strike the eagle wish and condor need,
And whose fixation is of now and past
Thrusts changing stars within my future's seed.

I am that man whose hour and place are heat.
The candles in the rivers of the blood
Gutter upon their individual waves
Till the red beacons of the heart are lit
To burn the brittle and impassive lives.

And you are heat, who are my place and hour,
For in those crossed diagonals of the mind
Breeds the event and bitter leaf of change,
And on the fell immortal tree and star
You are the doomful angel of my rage,

Of whom conflagrant sears the vitriol flow,
Western the winds are salt, the thunder ice,
And interlacing seas throb in my blood.
So you, the starry and tellural now
Plait hour and place, my evil and my good.

Hurley

Leaving the woods where flowers are permanent,
Iced for ever in the neutral brain,
We lay in the field torn by the tractor's heel
And watched the valley green with April and rain.
Supine under the sun, we were divine
In hilled detachment from the Easter scene.

Model were Hurley's houses, its torpid men
Insects on the glittering leather road.
The beautiful plane was devilish as it swooped
Shadowing death on the unwilling field,
But good and evil were enemy and far
Where height upheld us from perennial war.

We only were permanent as remembered flowers,
Shunning that hour the perpetual death of time.
Happiness made us great as the skeleton trees,
Older than chalk and young as the green lime.
Our nearness sprouted in grass beneath our bones.
Our kinship was lasting as infrangible stones.

Rural Poem

Blue hyphens, tiny dragons that desire
Raises from wretched ponds in love's hot flight
To soar as double in the bluer sky
Deepen my torture of unwilling sight.

Here are the pleasant place and pleasant hour,
The friendly bouncing girl, the quilted peace
Smothering the age's multiplying terror;
Here is the nightfall living, like a face.

Yet, even here, remote from the familiar,
Far from your shape or the associate fact,
I feel beyond new place and the new faces
The angry need castrated of the act.

I feel the evening that has never known you
Wilt on a landscape that you never trod.
Playing the social man, the clown for strangers,
I know my love is immanent and god.

And, as the marble angel on the tomb,
Pointing his trumpet, calls the heart to grief,
You, distant, are the warning in my pleasure,
That shows the death at wait in flesh and leaf.

So, rocky seeming though the pious elms,
Warm though the tentative hand upon the skin,
I know this place is false, I know defeat
And lust's humiliation stain the screen.

The azure insects rise on glassy wings,
Brittle and weak, united selves of love.
They have no other world beyond their sight.
My shame is their serene and upward drive.

Dry Drayton

The Real Stranger

You are that real stranger of my day
Who walks about my mind, undoes each door
Long shut with dust, opens the sleeping eye
And drives away the nibbling rats of fear.

You are the flame for which I waited long
To set a fire within the lazy heart
And thaw the frozen hinges of the brain.
You are life's wheel and time's reviving heat.

Within the muscle of your mental arm
My urge exists and is propelled through time
To pass the mirrored circle of its edge
Into the darkness where night's banners stream

Black with destruction for an evil age.
You are my strength, the heart behind my pulse,
The lung behind my breath. From you I live
A stranger to my past, to all my selves

That posed and wept across my days the foe.
And so made new within your strength I rise
A second man, and in your beauty know
My end, and my beginning in your eyes.

Song for the South

Beyond the islands where my knees are set
In solitary snow, in rock and ice,
Lay out your south in sands of wine and heat,
In hills of drowsy hands and sad olive trees.

Surrender so all ripeness of your fruit,
Pomegranate-coloured warmth, down youth on peach,
Purple of pulp, the intricate flowering sweet
Soft fig pouting to the greedy reach.

Be in mind's Avignon the dropping night,
Winter where swallows are immune from frost,
And where nemonic artifices shout
The inarticulate blood within your breast.

So from your heart let the slow stalks of ease
Bind round my solitude the briar of peace.

Laying Your Hand

Laying your hand on the pectoral tendon,
Closing the flickering eye with lips
Soft as sensation, O do not remember
The anatomical atlas of death
Spread under skin for the scalpel sight.

Sweeping your stroke on the flexile muscle,
Touching the nerve to anxious fire,
Do not recall the crying voices
That star the cities, O do not think
Of the angry metal that may condemn us.

Only, remember, the instant is lovely,
Only the pointed place is true.
Locking our separateness in love
We dare not heed the crying voices,
We dare not dream of the falling cities.

For the angry metal that may condemn us,
The voice that accuses, walls that crush
Live in another world and evening.
Their shadows fall on the real moment
But only the lovable flesh is true.

Rippling Stone

This hand has passed and like a rippling stone
Whorls your white shadow in the clearing glass,
And now I feel and dare not know you lean

Upon my rigid arm like one who goes
For long or ever, your words almost the last.
Soon your speech and louder silence will cease.

Soon the ears will be void and the glass erased,
Soon the doorways will empty as you leave,
Soon I shall throw your flowers out like grass.

The margin of my need you would not fill
And in that incompletion of your gift
Your going cancels little that I will,

Yet you once moored me from the ebbing drift
That tides my now upon an oarless craft.

The Fountain at Vaucluse

Many years in sentimental willing exile
Petrarch walked beside the inky waters,
Posing the gentle rebel and inconsolable lover,
Expecting laurels and extolling Laura
In the sickly voice of an emotion long dead.

Meanwhile, in Avignon, married and virtuous,
Laura had brats, grew matronly and fat,
And worshipped strictly under the Papal shadow.
She hardly thought of Petrarch beside the inky waters
And died respected for every homely virtue.

After her death he left the enigmatic waters
And returned to the jaded valley at Avignon,
Where, under the Papal shadow and the cicada,
The laurels fell on his lined and lofty brow.

Windows

Windows from which the captains stepped to death,
Climbing from time on condemnation's tear,
Borne on the breath of boys beyond their fear,
Above illusion and hate's human heat;

Windows at which the girls left life for love,
Stepping in joy to indecisive fate;
Windows at which the burning sang too late
To shun the end death's salamanders live;

All windows open in those fluid ports
That are your eyes, where shadow armies roll
Constricted in destruction, rulers fall
Like walls in earthquake, all ambitions wane
As in Les Baux the fig trees break and part
The dying town where grass seeps in again.

Binaries

1

"We are all lonely," you said
at dreamtime out of death,
from which I must conclude
that being dead
is as private a matter
as dying
or living

2

Lady believe
your sixteen summers bracing at the blouse
too tight for blowsiness,
that old man's look of rage
is lust, not anger,
is lust's despair, not love.

3

Soul, clap your hands,
    But do not sing;
Your angel flies
    On raven wing.

4

Some need write no poems
since they are.
Others, who are not,
must write.

You —

    and I.

5

The sunburst of urgency on your face,
and my mood, cold as a snowdrift!

I burn now in the hell of memory.

The End Man

Ballad of the End Man

On that day skeletons from all cupboards
Emerged, shouting the past, pointing the derogatory finger.

Among ghosts also the rising was universal,
Not one keeping his post to guard an evil tradition.

The rulers were nonplussed by this insurrection,
For the dead were immune from poison gas or gun.

At eight o'clock the massacre began,
The slaughter of the living by guilt and confusion.

Some went mad. Some stood their ground. Most fled
Into the last wild woods along the marches.

Nestlings and still-born lambs became our foods,
Our houses piles of boulders thatched with reeds,

While the victorious rioted in our homes,
Eating the Oxford Marmalade, lapping the wines.

For us there was no rest in our misfortune,
No sanctuary immune from death's deathless vision.

And one by one they have found each hiding place
And wormed out the hidden. I am the last of my race.

So spoke the last man, as he became a ghost,
Received in triumph by the spectral host.

The Tower

Last night the sappers halted. Under my house
Their tapping ceased. The silence deafened with fear
As I saw through earth the shifting eye of the fuse.

As timed the mine's jet rose. In the explosion
Seven died. But I, the sought man, fled
Into the hills, this roofless tower's seclusion.

Babel above me, to the metallic sky
Stone funnels. Gaps in the crumbling wall
Show the peaceful village and the cold sea.

The hovels are stone, warm when night is dry.
Matted thistles uphold the caving thatch
And sheeted iron denotes prosperity.

Here seems no gold of sun or coin to seek,
No prey or promise for owl or limping fox,
But gain only for the man seeking peace.

Yet the prophetic sounds in my brain domed
Expand to fill the quiet of the sky
With the tap in the tunnel and the winged hum.

For here, I know, my enemies' saps will creep,
Pushed to explosive ends, and to new dens
I shall restage the skin-of-teeth escape.

Time and again I shall repeat the act,
Fear and relief and fear, as every hour
March the soulless figures of the zodiac clock.

To Simone Saint-Sabin
at Sacré Coeur, 1938

One day when fallen are these icy domes
That mock Byzantium, and this teeming hill's
Land for the plough like Carthage, spades will come
Probing like surgeons under the sheep's kale.

And in the tin museum among the folds
Stooping archaeologists with black beards
Will piece the glasses found in the Rue Pigalle,
Index the wine corks and the visiting cards.

If I can stand then under this white wall
I shall see your looks fall over vanished Paris
As you tell your old tale of the Virgin and her roses,
Ignoring the Commune and its wall's blood of many.

I shall also hear you shout in another hour:
"I would stand behind a mitrailleuse for France!"
And wonder at you and that lost love of land
Whose verbal glory spelt with dots from guns.

The Last Man

There is an only challenger to his kingdom.
Through the faint ruin of paddy field and vine
The last man, conscious of finality,
Climbs, carrying history like a shell.

Slow is the hour when, Selkirk of a world,
His lonely mind surveys a fragment realm
Of manless cities where the rats remain.
The remnants of his reign, the iron toys
Left from the past, shine with the perished eyes
Of his deciduous comrades. Theirs his end
Waits on the mountain with his only foe,
The shadow that will smile and be himself
When falls his ash to the residual us
As Arctic time assaults the senile world.

Spoken In Love

Spoken in love, no new vernacular
Rises this season from the heart
Through the breaking images, the secular
Figures of toil or sport.

Love in this season, as unicorn fabulous
feeds in countries far away.
Under the passionate heart and the sedulous
Manner the heart is clay.

So in this spring when canker autumnal
Lies as seed in the breaking bud
Deeds are sterile and ice perpetual
Sets pain in the slow blood.

Caught on the Hop

Mercury ebbs in the sterile tubes
    When Death, the god with the eyeless socket,
    With ice in his heart and fire in his pocket,
Enters and fuses the wires and the bulbs.

The rats and the birds on the telegraph wires
    Saw his arrival and made their escape.
    But we who were watching the news on the tape
Saw not the lights dim or sinking fires.

We're caught on the hop — too late to depart.
    Death, with his knives and his satchels of bombs
    Opens the door and strides through the rooms
With fire in his pocket and ice in his heart.

At This Hour

Record that at this hour decisions are made
Whether to plant the dragon in the shade,
Whether to write or let the offer slide,
Whether to breed, and who shall be the bride?

Record that cricketers are shedding pads
As farmers scatter their last rain of seeds,
And in the hills the clouds are signed with red
For men to die after the ore has bled.

Record that flanges are straining at the rail
And planes are anxious to shed their monstrous hail,
The wolf is waiting and the worm in egg
Grows for the Attic face and runner's leg.

The Bones of Love

Who can record the street's temptation?
I crush the dry bones underfoot
And the devil's instruction bubbles through blood.
The word is annihilation.

We burn as children die in arms.
The devil's word within our hearts
Whirls in a gyroscope of fire.
The dry bones break in many forms.

The stones reject the foot of love.
The devil's gospel in the stones
Breaks the age and breaks the bones.
Day's eyelid closes on the grave.

The Green Moat of Time

Time, a green moat around the castled mind,
Holds corpses in its depth, that rise and sink
On tides of thought, stirred by the blind
Currents among the weeded shadows of the brink.

Bound hand and foot, their bloated bodies float
Sometimes under battlements where the watcher stands;
Their eyes are eaten by fishes, their grey cheeks wet
With slime where their hair creeps in weedy strands.

Yet in those dead features the watcher sees
A moment live across the wasted faces,
When the lips become red and vanished eyeballs rise
And the swollen tongue speaks thickly and accuses.

And as such bodied memories sink and fade,
Leaving their ripples on the closing slime,
The watcher turns within the walls, to hide
His dread of failure and his fear of time.

Doomed Habitations

Looking into the windows that doom has broken
Where the vague star illumines death and dust
And the shadows of actions whose ends are forsaken
Stir under the falling walls, senile and lost;

And looking into the doorways where unspoken names
Shine and distintegrate on the rotting plaques,
Surviving their owners who have left like dreams,
Sinking into the past as sea-sucked wrecks;

Remember, stranger, that here men grew and worked,
Loved and were angry, and in general lived
Peaceable lives till one day, spitted on their brothers' knives,
Stuck to the curdling heart by nails they loved,
They died in horror and their towns were left,
And rotted, buried under the dust and leaves.

Speech from the Dock

You who of empty worlds are denizen,
Livers in time who sleep in broken hell,
Or speak the dying languages of pain;
You whom the burning hours transmit no bell;

And you whose far and lovely fatherland
Lives beyond future and the final star,
Whose battling journeys tell no happy end
Seen in horizons where the ideal are;

As on this bitter breath of night we ride
Across a time we cannot turn away
Into a spurious past or future burning red,
I ask you — forget your dreams and live today.

No clock, once turned, ticks the same hour again,
No time runs straight the route of our desire.
Our yearnings to the past are calls in vain;
Towards no future can our charts be sure.

It is only in now our hope can ever live,
Where past and future are absorbed and blent.
Only in now the sick can ever love
And the lost art achieve its occident.

After the Star

The breeding clouds eclipsed that country's sun.
Each year the sentimental edifices
Grew green as moss upon the sodden plain
Of the ageing mind, and the token faces
That are never old moved in the wearing rain.

It was a day of death to enter in that land,
Each day another death for the lapsing soul
Among the breasty hills, beyond the whispering sand.
There were no voices, and the air was still,
And the flitting women were lame, and deaf, and blind.

For over all that country ruled the enigma.
Life had no answer, death not any end
In the untitled valley's weeping summer.
The meagre trees, swept by a silent wind
Lingered like spectres by the Lethean river.

This was the land where our desires had led,
This the dim Hades of unspeaking want,
Where there was no more evil, no more good.
Into a prison of mist the sky was bent
Over the dead earth on which we stood.

The Second Country

The used symbols, island, now and white,
Will not survive into this second country,
Nor will the mask of shipwrecked or explorer
Confer the seal and visa on my entry.

I cannot colour this land or time the hour
Or say if the rocks are really insular,
Or clothe myself as the poet or the lover,
Or fit the mobile mask of the casual caller.

For this place, I see, is ruled by the enigma.
It is not white, or black, or any colour,
Nor is its time in present, past or future,
Nor is its form isle or peninsular.

Shaped as the sphinx are all its silent mountains;
Impassive as card players' are all faces,
All bodies Protean, no and every form
In the unliving day that never ceases.

There is not any love within this country,
Nor breed its hills the power of fear or wonder.
Only, I know, its symbol is the question
That time will make a final death to answer.

Destroyers

Under the climbing hill, under the loam and the bark
Creeping and undermining are the destroyers,
The evil rat and the mole, the grub and the beetle
Eating the void behind the impervious surface,
Parching the sap behind the bud and the leaf.

Under the long breasts of the sea, under the lake and the puddle
Swimming and ever searching are the destroyers,
The shark and the hag, torpedo and the leech,
Biting the hollows where the swimmer fails,
Sucking the virgin blood and the bestial substance.

Under the crinkling flesh, under the breasts and the eyes,
Moving and ever attacking are the destroyers,
The worm and the fluke, bacillus and the virus,
Boring the flesh and clamping on the vitals,
Breaking the blood and softening the bone.

Under the thoughtful mind and the careful thought
Burning and disintegrating are the destroyers,
Love and greed, hatred and always desire,
Turning the wish and breaking the idea,
Distorting the intention in the deed.

Under the soil and the water, under the flesh and the spirit,
Living and multiplying are the destroyers.
In the day I hear their palpable motion
Working the clay and air, and feel them within me
In the dead evening rotting the bone and the spirit.

Epitaph for a Double Tragedy

Because our fact was darker than the legend,
Because we breathed beyond the act of living,
Because we spoke with hearts cut out and eaten,
Time must condemn who have no easy living.

Song

Time's destroying claws
scatter sand and soil,
crush the seed and the bulb,
but in the brain's damp earth
memory evades the dog.

So our thought has still
beauty grudging smiles,
deeds boy heroes did,
anger and the thin
residue left by death.

And as skeleton leaves
live again in frost
we shall keep for age
folly and bitterness
and disillusion's itch.

Snow Pike and Tarn

Across the wide scene of the mountain world,
Snow pike and tarn, green pasture slopes before,
Black horses race, their manes in anger swirled,
Breaking the shaggy turf and scattering sheep with fear.

The 'bus sways on across the broken uplands,
Bearing me away from cragged and lofty winter,
Till, through the passes and beyond the islands
I shall walk into plains where cities throb like thunder,

Where, under the shadow of the mechanical ape,
The great are forsaken and the fear of the unreal
Magnifies the mean. Observing the evil shape
Of the weak made hard within their gloomy wheel,

I shall remember how black horses race,
Spirits of strength across the mountain sky;
Thus, living through the mechanical haze,
The rejected move, creating their own country.

Circle of Mirrors

Self

Always the circle of mirrors is unbroken.
I am the person encountered at every turn
Like the lead penny or perpetual ghost.

It is easy to stay. It would be easier to go
If I were not the circle. The mirrors grow
To fingers cutting off the friendly west,

And each finger is myself as a stranger,
Distorted to a grey saint or sinister lounger.
It is myself I must break to leave the circle.

It is myself I must break if I am to leave
Temperate west and live the skipped age
Where the lips are not fettered or the heart single.

But it is so easy to stay in the sloth I hate,
Dreading and desiring always to meet
The real stranger who will light my day.

It is so easy to wait for the mirrors to crack
Instead of smashing and risking the ache
Of myself broken to set a future free.

And yet before the enveloping circle knit
Rigid in sphere to hold heart's head and foot
I must apply the hammer to the glass

And break reflections of my evil ring
Till, free of mirrored selves, my self like spring
Shall rise from ice to turn the living keys.

Memorandum From Arcadia

I in Arcadia lived. I have traced on stone
    The record of cold days, and scratched on glass
    The seismograph's stutter (Time would erase
Figures on paper or iron, would rot even bone).

For hunters I have shown the tracks of deer
    With bent boughs, cairns and tablets nailed on trees.
    I have marked the levels of the inland seas,
And watched the salmon courting at every weir.

I have experimented with foodstuffs, eaten snails
    And nettles (finding the latter tough).
    I have found the water clear and tasty enough.
I have kept the wolves from the hut with wooden rails.

Explorers who follow me into the hut will find
    Blankets and sheets, matches on the table,
    Tins of food, a wrecked launch's cable,
A telephone directory, a white stick for the blind.

I shall do the thing the neatest and cleanest way.
    Cord rots soon. I shall drop to the floor.
    I shall be found behind the kitchen door
Sprawling untidily on the trodden clay.

Solitary

Time gutters like a leaking tap
On lonely waiting for the phones to ring
In one-rooms of home where gas taps wait
For tired fingers to loose Lethe like song.

And I am with those solitary in small hells,
Watching their acts as if my shadow moved,
Knowing in them the glasses of a life
When without you my life too shall have died.

For all is potential in us: boredom and fear,
The undefeatable dread of naked selves,
And hope surviving, tenuous, to the hour
When the hand turning inward ends and saves.

Stories About A

Where shall I wear your knife? Shall I wear it in my throat?
　　Shall I wear it where the orator his jeer, the actor his kiss?
Shall I use it to cut grass or cake, or to scrape
　　White off blind men's sticks or grease off keys?

I shall scratch the mystic circle in imaginary colours,
　　And write stories about A. and the tenth card.
I shall cut the eyes out of idols and the buds from elms.
　　But where shall I wear your knife? Was it meant for the heart?

Words From the Tulip Throat

When words flow from the tulip throat
And on the silent sap towards the brain
Spreads in clear morning spring's insidious thought;

When transient peace falls cool as early rain
On dusty minds grown weary for the light
In dry worlds where death's dark stars shine;

When in the human flower the gentle feet
Tread soft petals and the searching tongue
Thrusts its pollen to love's sleeping seed;

Then soar the heart's loud drones with flight like song
Passing as princes through the friendly skies,
Fed on our toil and hourly growing strong,

Till, chosen, in love's last twin flight they rise
And give both seed and selves in life's destroying cause.

He

As in a valley swirled snow
Coils, emblems to his view
Spiral to sky flow.

Blade, bed, hearse, the nerves of pain
Are not.

       But grey sand to groyne
Piled, dust from harrow, snarl
Of weasel, bracken snaked curl,
Veined sorrel cup, yellow
Crown or coltsfoot, hollow
Rat's home in rotted willow . . .

Till, as time caught in amber
Mind rots in skull's chamber.

Wider Than Clouds

Wider than clouds and more serene,
Higher than mountains and more sheer,
Night on the evening's sombre green
Angels of my despair appear.

These constant overshadowers
Who blur the sun with towering heads
Are my peculiar foes and followers
And are more true and older than all friends.

Clasped in the darkness of their misty wings
Lies all my life, the journey and the clock,
Under their snowy breasts my raven sings
And in their fleshless hands my visions break.

Unto the end I know their august flight
Will follow all my steps, the streets and hills
Of love, the sorrow and delight,
Till their wings cover me as evening falls.

Prologue

Remembering
Hardy and Yeats
singing again
in the last years
I knew
muteness would end.
Survival was all.

I thought
singing again
I would celebrate
living things,
birds
and animals whom I prefer
mostly to men,
the green earth
that renews my mind,
and those moments
epiphanous
when the light
transfigures a landscape
and transvalues.

Yet now
my voice hurries
down the green valleys,
between the incandescent mountains,
and under the sonorous clouds
of swirling snow geese,
jays, gulls and eagles,
ignoring them all
to sing of death
and the dark love
that grows in
death's dark shadow
like the purple blossom
of soldanella
thawing its way
up through the radiant
snow.

Notes on Visitations

Sometimes
when I am alone
the music strikes
and I sing
with confidence and ease
the increasingly complex
melodies
of Mozart's
never lived
and final years.

Or the rhythm
enters my limbs
and I step
like a Greek sailor,
companion of Odysseus,
prancing with
elephantine joyful
solemnity and without
benefit of chroeography
between my books, my
manuscripts piled high
as obsolescent
obstacles
to dancing.

Or I am seized
with glossolaliac
motions
and the verses
stutter out
in metric order
and a new tongue,
unknown yet obvious
with meaning.
This occurs
walking in woods.
But always
when the fit strikes
I am alone,
walls down, gates
open and always
the pending onrush
of joy
lifts into ecstasy
of limbs
gyrating
or tumbling
unsilenceable
voice.

Such visitations
possessed me at sixteen
and at sixty
the gods
revisit.

The Mountain Road

Mirror, mirror, at the road's bend,
Tell me where the trail will end;
Tell me where my feet take flight
Out of shadow into light;
Tell me where my soul takes breath
Into living out of death.

Found Fictions

The found object, the *trouvaille,* was a great preoccupation among the Surrealists whose influence spilled belatedly into England during the 1930's when I was a young poet working there. Visually, the fascination with the *trouvaille* has continued, in conceptual art and other latter-day offshoots of Dada and Surrealism, but in literature the preoccupation with the found has tended to become restricted to whatever is already there in writing and preferably in print. One finds a poem sleeping in prose, and by arranging it into lines and stanzas produces a poem — and sometimes a good one. In recent years in Canada John Robert Colombo and F. R. Scott have been perhaps the most successful at this kind of discovery.

But there is another kind of finding, also favoured by the Surrealists in their time, and occurring sporadically throughout literature (Coleridge's "Kubla Khan" being perhaps the most celebrated example) but recently rather neglected. That is the dream. Here and there writers use dreams to emphasize themes in novels; the prophetic dreams in Orwell's *1984* are examples. And many writers, without avowing it, produce fictions that seem to be derived from dreams; I have always thought this was the origin of most of Kafka's short parables and sketches, which have all the condensation, vividness and wry logic of dream fictions.

In general, however, we seem nowadays to view our dreams too clinically; Freud and Jung between them have induced us to regard as symptoms what in fact are often imaginative structures in their own rights, works of art waiting to be recognized. I shall shortly present a number of dreams that did in fact lend themselves to immediate transmission into literary form. Like most people, I usually experience dreams that may be structured when they are taking place but which are remembered fragmentarily and chaotically, so that by the time I try to write them down whatever coherence they may have had is frayed beyond recapture. But at all periods in my life I have also had landmark dreams that have often stayed in my mind more clearly and vividly than episodes in the world of actuality. My earliest detailed memory is of a recurrent dream I experienced at the age of four. During childhood I would dream so vividly of places where I had never actually been that the experience would seem to be part of a real memory, to such an extent that in adolescence I would work laboriously at disentangling what had really taken place from the dream world for whose actual existence I could find no evidence, despite the vividness with which that visionary country would linger in my mind. Once I did disconcertingly enter in waking life the exact counterpart of a landscape I had known in dream; this happened when I went to Holland for the first time in 1946 at the age of 34, and found myself living in a farmhouse among dykes and artificial lakes of which I had dreamed, without then having seen them, when I was a boy of thirteen. This is no place to try and explain such a recognition. The point to be made is that certain dreams form themselves in such ways that on waking they can be recognized as the material for poems or fictions; in fact, are found poems or found fictions.

The four found fictions I am about to tell are all parables as well as dreams, and they have a common element, the fact that they take place on trains. Whatever deep significance the train may have as a symbolic vehicle (and that will become naturally evident in the telling), I should say that a great deal of my earlier life was spent on trains or connected with railways. My maternal and paternal grandfathers and my father all worked for the old Great Western Railway in England, and I put in eleven years as a clerk in the railway's engineering department, first in the Paddington head office and later as office manager for large makework construction projects during the later 1930's. Each day I would travel by train up to London and back from the small Thameside town where I lived. On trains I made friends, encountered lovers, talked, gambled, read and wrote poems, day after day, year after year, and so the railway became part of my leisure as well as my working life. It therefore seems to me entirely natural that the archetypal questing should in my mind take the form of a train journey.

I give the four found or given fictions in the order of dreaming.

I

It is the night when I have a heavy heart attack and am taken to the Vancouver General Hospital, feeling very deep in the valley of the shadow and wondering whether I shall still be alive next morning. I go into a morphine-aided sleep, and almost at once am aware of the motion of a train, the clack-a-clack of wheels running over an imperfect railbed. I open my eyes and realize that I am lying in a bunk in a railway carriage, all mahogany and brass fittings, like the coaches that in the 1960's still survived the British era on the railways of Malaysia and Ceylon. I let up the window blind; the train is travelling, with a great sense of hurrying to make up for lost time, beside an immensely wide river between ranges of tropically forested hills which I recognize as the Upper Mekong, towards the border of Tibet. I get up and dress; the train's urgency communicates itself to me. I become aware, without being told, that I am the only passenger on the train; it is running for me. As soon as I have got dressed and packed my night bag, I realize the train is slowing down; I look out of the window and see we are approaching a long wharf beside which a glittering white ferry boat is lying, steam up. I open the door and in my eagerness leap out of the train before it has stopped, but as my feet touch the platform, the ferry steamer emits a reproachful whistle and swings away from the wharf. I watch the white ship ploughing through the waters to the other shore, whose pagodas glitter like the gilded temples of Pagan. I feel immense regret, immense relief. I climb back into the train, which starts up at once to take me I know not where.

II

Again, I am in a train travelling at high speed. It lurches and swings so much that I find it hard to avoid falling as I walk along the central corridors, on each side of which there are not passenger compartments, but large bins filled with trunks, parcels and mail bags, thrown together hiddledy-piggledy. Overalled attendants are rather lacksadaisically sorting them, and at the end of each coach is a cubicle where clerks sit writing in ledgers.

One of the overalled workers stops me and asks what I am doing on the train. I answer that I want to get from X to Y. "This is a baggage train", says the man; "passengers are forbidden." "But I still want to get from X to Y," I answer in a surge of anger. "Do you have a permit to travel on the baggage train?" he asks. "No, but I still want to get from X to Y." He takes me firmly by the arm. "It is not allowed for passengers without permits to travel on this train," he shouts. "You are breaking the regulations and I must take you to the train master."

The train master is a tall fat man, with a regal dignity permeating his massiveness, rather like the king of Tonga, and a genial though clearly ironic look on his face. He tells me quietly that for boarding the train without authority I am subject to trial and imprisonment. I repeat, with what even to me seems now a ludicrously monotonous insistence: "But I want to go from X to Y."

He stands in silence for a moment, looking intently into my eyes. His smile is that of a Gandhara Buddha. "Have you a watch?" he says. "Yes." "Give it to me." I trust him instinctively and take off my gold wrist watch. He looks at it, opens the back, and takes out a wheel. "You keep the watch," he says, handing it back to me. "I shall keep the wheel. Time has stopped. One day we will meet again. Then we will put the watch and the wheel together, and time will start once more."

III

I am going abroad, and start out from my old Thameside town of Marlow to catch a boat train. At Marlow station my father's former colleagues tell me there is congestion on the main line; I should go by a devious route, north to High Wycombe, then southeast through Uxbridge, which I do. As in all dreams, the journey is telescoped, and despite the great detour I arrive quickly at the station from which the boat train is due to leave.

The station is a warren of corridors and offices, with a frustrating lack of signs, and it takes me a long time to find the right ticket counter and, when I have booked my seat, even longer to reach the platform from which the train will leave.

But eventually I board the gigantic train, whose coaches have the breadth and height of the cabin of a 747 plane. By now I am seeking a mysterious companion, but though the first coaches are crowded I see no sign of him. I meet a conductor whom I seem to know. "Have you seen him?" I ask. "No, he isn't on the train." "I'm sure he is," I insist, and we walk on until we reach what seems a completely empty carriage. About halfway down it I see, above a seat-back, the head of the only occupant. "I told you he would be here," I say to the conductor.

At the sound of my voice, my self rises from his seat and greets me: "You see, I've found a completely empty coach!" Then we embrace — I and I — and go arm-in-arm towards the splendidly appointed dining car which is next to the coach.

IV

Again I am seeking a boat train, and come to a station which I am told is Victoria. It is quite unlike the Victoria of the waking world, or any other railway station in my experience; it consists of a maze of flagged passages in which tiny booths are secreted, with no sign of platforms or railway tracks. I go up to one of the booths, where a pretty ash-blonde girl is sitting. I tell her I want a ticket to Paris. She asks me the time of the train. I ask her to book me on the earliest possible departure. "You must tell me which — the number and the time," she says. "Can't *you* tell me the times of the trains?" I ask. "I am here only to issue tickets," she says; "passengers must find out the times of the trains for themselves." "But there are no timetables on the boards," I complain; "where can I find them?"

"I will show you where," she says, and with that she comes out of her little office, locks it, and, taking me by the hand, goes before me — her bell of yellow hair like a beacon — across the paved courtyards until we come to a series of stone stairways that rise up through gardens of shrubs and mosses to a large building that, when we enter, looks like an old-fashioned club in India. An elderly man is sitting at a desk, and as soon as I go in he shouts, stentorianly: "Here comes old George, going hand in hand!" I stride up angrily, shouting: "Who the bloody hell are you? How do you know me?" He picks up a copy of the *Times* with a photograph on the front page, and for a moment I think it must be me; it is of him, and it bears the name "Charles Madge" beneath it. I look with surprise at the poet-friend of my youth, born in the same year as I, and cannot see in him the dark, spare, youthful figure I remember. But the blonde girl is pulling at my hand, and we go on, join a table of young people, some of whom I recognize as my former students, and drink, talk and laugh until I uneasily remember my train. "You can phone from here," says the blonde girl. "Victoria Station — Enquiries." She points to a phone booth, but when I go in I find that the immense directory goes no farther than C. I go back to the table. The girl reaches out, takes my hand, strokes. "Sit down. Be calm. The train has gone already. You were not meant to catch it."

*　　*　　*

I have not discussed these dreams with Freudians. Jungians tell me
they are integration dreams, which may be true; they also warn me
to beware of the charming little anima in Dream IV. What interests
me most is the power of the sleeping mind to shape such enigmatic
artifacts, such carefully structured found fictions — or should we
call them "given"?

Anima, or,
Swann Grown Old

The anima
is a dream denizen.
When she incarnates
to enter one's life,
archetype infesting
an actual person,
look out! You are being
haunted by yourself,
and when the anima
retreats to its darkness
and the woman
lapses into
platitude, you
will find a whole
province of memory
annexed to the dream;
under its raven flags
lost to reality.

Bone and Skin

Sorrow
has whittled you
to the bone and skin
of lasting,
worn at your black
and frightening beauty,
made you accessible.

As you run up the steps
offering to my kiss
instead of your face
that mask
of an incredible nun,
whose great eyes
look through and
beyond
and yet include
me in their vast pain,
I know there has been
a change in the weather
of love.

I am too old
to expect
what I desired with
such dumb terror,
but know the tenderness
of touching
solitudes
and I accept,
granting romantic dogma
that the best love
is satisfied
never.

Party Dress

You walk as queens
should but do
only in Celtic
dream-tales
and wear your glad-rags
with the austere's
audacity, your face
an ikon set in
a splendour of vulgarity
self-transcendent.

I remember
how the deities
of Phidias
whom we see now as
all perma-ice,
were painted once in
tints that vibrated,
screaming to eyeballs
in cool temple shadows
messages
from a realm beyond
taste and proportion, beyond
sense and spirit, where
all things in their
innate vividness
are themselves,
discordant, yet
in that ultimate
equilibrium
harmonious.

Taurus to Pisces

I shall never gore
your skittering silver.
A heron
in the shallows
would stab you;
even a bear
would scoop you
from the pebbles,
but a clumsy ruminant
must stand and
from his dripping muzzle
bellowing
see you hide in
the weedbed's shadows
and know that even if
like a hippopotomus
he chewed through
to the end
you would still dart,
a rippling knife,
into the next concealment.

And if I ask
the water-bearer
to empty
the whole lake,
I shall see you
gasping in mud,
your silver fading,
and know you
still
elude me.

Black Epiphanies

I dread those
rare and
black
epiphanies
when your face sets
in the rigour
of anger and
in your Scutari
you become Nightingale
posing as
stern daughter
of the voice of God,
but also
as the implacable fire
burns all sweetness
out of your beauty,
black-haired Hecate
helmed with fury.

Days later
I still apprehend
your shadowing
my thoughts,
a raven angel.

And then slip back to
the ambiguities
of daylight
when you are again
gay, comprehensible,
ordinary and beloved,

and I remember
that the Errinyes
were part-time protectors
and that ravens
transitively also
feed.

Sonnets on Human Beauty

I

The beautiful, as you experience,
live only in the magic of reflection,
in the sharp breath, the halted glance
of man faced with the seeming of perfection;

or in the mirror, lying fortune-teller
showing the right for left of their true natures,
see, since eyes and glasses show no clearer,
dimly the soul behind their splendid features.

And so live in unsureness with themselves,
distrusting those who praise, and yet assuming
praise is their right, humble and proud at once,
and caught, like kings who are their subjects' slaves,
within time's wheel, for charm — like power — declining
frees them to bleak, belated innocence.

II

But see the same in the beholder's eye;
view what chameleon acts the brilliant mask
of being beautiful demands. It is variety
keeps beauty's stillness living. There's a task

for drama. This morning you're a queen in tragedy,
tomorrow a pretty clown, and then a saint,
and then a model mother, and next day
a practical woman, brittle and efficient

and always dazzling. Hedda and Deirdre,
Arletty, Mrs. Warren, Jocasta and Saint Joan —
I've known you do them all across a room
for two or three to watch. Twixt acts your self I'd see
confused, a little stupid with pretence, alone,
and pity how your beauty was your doom.

Blaze of Azaleas

A cold spring day
in the blaze of azaleas.
Walking near your home
I remember
in their wisdom
ancient Chinese
wrote tenderly their
poems of old
men in love.
They understood
the atmospherics of
ripeness and the
cloudy agony
of voiceless
longing.

Cyclops

Since true love's eyes are in two bodies set
his love's a Cyclops, caverned and unknown,
in grief a monster grown, one-eyed,
one-legged as well, one-armed, one-eared,
no honoured casualty, but from birth
stumbling, uncouth, myope,
and mockable, and mocked.
Yet of one mind
and single-hearted.

Gist of a Sonnet

Dark lady, you are
eating my heart out
with teeth of silence.

Chinese Torture

Every day
is a small
cut in a
long death as
I await
your voice say-
ing nothing.

Essence

The essence of mothhood
is in circling the lamp
before it is lit.

Lopped Hand

Remembering
is the ache
of an amputation.
The lopped hand
still pains.

Green Grass and Sea

The grass is so green that
geese should be pecking there,
and the sun shines level and
honey-gold on the riders
strolling their horses
back to the stables. It
is the suspended moment,
time singing in a bright
still rush from day
to evening. I
stand empty and
receiving, already
joyful, when the car
surges beside me
like a boat backing water.
My heart jolts at the
hit of a girl's face,
apricot in that
brightness, gold
cowling hair and great
eyes green as the sea.
The car sails on,
the instant
ends, process continues
and colours ebb from
the darkening meadows,
from my eyes.

Next day in Safeway
sheepishly I stand, a
stale loaf in my hand.
I offer my quarter.
The girl looks at me. I
drown in that
green sea.

Sonnet for Marie

(from Pierre de Ronsard)

As on the May month's bough the rose I see,
In the sweet joy of its first blossoming,
Make the sky jealous with its blazonry
When dawn upon its leaves wet tears does fling,
And grace and love in its smooth calyx rest
Balming the groves and gardens fragrantly,
Yet beaten by the rain or sun's high zest,
Petal on petal bruised ope languidly:
    So in your first and freshest novelty
    When earth and heaven envied your beauty,
    Fate took your life and ashes now you lie.
    For requiem my sobs and tears receive,
    This crock of milk, baskets with flowers piled high,
    For you were the flesh of roses, whether you live or die.

Rondeau

(from Charles d'Orleans)

The season casts his gear
Of wind and rain and cold,
And clothes himself in gold
Of sunlight bright and clear.
No beast or bird I hear
That sings not free and bold;
The season casts his gear
Of wind and rain and cold.
The rills and rivers steer
Their silver waves and gold;
In brilliancy untold
Each changes with the year.
The season casts his gear.

Dialogue Between
A Poor Poet and the Author

(from Ponce-Denis Ecouchard Lebrun)

Someone has robbed me!
   — I weep for your grief!
All of my verses!
   — I weep for the thief!

Epitaph

(from Paul Scarron)

He who lies beneath this spot
Died full oft ere hence he passed.
Make no noise, and wake him not;
Here poor Scarron sleeps at last.

Grey About the Ears

(from Anacreon)

I'm grey about the ears
and going thin on top.
What grace I had in youth
is rotting like my teeth.
I had sweet life before me.
Now it has passed me by.

Of course I lament it,
fearing what comes after.
It's a long way down to Hades
and the journey is dreadful.
And for him who has once gone down
there is never a climbing back.

At Thermopylae

(from Simonides)

Splendid was their fate who died here
and their death dark with beauty.
Their grave has become a shrine,
where lamentation turns into memory
and grief into glory.
Decay will not darken their name
nor will time that conquers all things.
This tomb of brave men holds
all Greece's glory. . . .

To a Girl

(from Sappho)

A peer of the gods he seems to me,
that happy man who sits beside you
listening quietly to the sweet cadence
of your voice, and to your laughter
that sets my heart trembling in my breast.
I look at you, just for a moment,
and I cannot speak. My tongue seems frozen
and yet I feel the fire tingling
under my skin. My eyes grow dim,
my ears are full of roaring,
the sweat pours down my trembling limbs;
I grow pale as the grass in winter
and swoon with love into a trance like death.

Lying Alone

(from Sappho)

The moon has gone down
and the Pleiades have set.
The night is half over.
I hear the midnight watch go by
and I lie alone.

The Year the Persians Came

(from Xenophanes)

Thus should we talk in winter
around the fire, with a strange guest among us,
all bellies satisfied, sweet wine beside us,
and filbert nuts to crack. Then we can speak.
"Pray tell us, sir, your name?
What was your home? How old are you?
How old were you in the year the Persians came?"

Remembering the Gods

(from Xenophanes)

Now we have swept the floor and washed our hands
we put fresh fragrant garlands on our heads,
and there the bowl stands waiting, brimmed with wine
scented like flowers and dulcet in its flavour.
The smoke of incense sanctifies the air,
and here the water's clean and cold as ice.
Brown bread and cheese and honey are to eat,
and there's a flower-strewn altar, and we sing.
We praise the god with pious words,
pour our libations, and we pray for strength
to act in righteousness and duty.
Then we can drink our fill, tell of fine deeds
and sing our jocund songs.
So long as we can keep from quarrelling
and safely find our pathway home
the gods will know that we remember them.

The Gods and God

(from Xenophanes)

The Ethiopian thinks his gods are black.
The Thracian sees them as blue-eyed, red-haired.
If cows and horses had hands as we do
and could draw and carve images
they would make gods like cows and horses.
But God is unlike beasts or men.
He is one, undifferentiated, undivided,
sees all, hears all, and without labour
sets all things in vibration
with a thought.

The Perfect Crown

(from Pindar)

When we are dead and gone away
how men speak of us is all
historians and poets have to go on.
So open-hearted Croesus is remembered
in all his generous grace,
but ruthless Phalaris who burnt men live
in the bronze bull of Sicily
they speak of with repulsion,
and so the poets chanting in the halls
have not a song for him.
He lives not in the dreams of boys.
Good fortune is the best of gifts;
the next is to be thought of gently.
Good fortune and good fame
give life its perfect crown.

(from Pythian I)

Men in Haste

(from Solon)

Everywhere you meet them, men in haste.
One man wanders over the fish-filled seas,
beaten by fearful winds, careless of life,
just in the hope of bringing home a profit.
Another ploughs his land, year after year,
curving his ploughshares twixt the loaded trees.
Others have learnt the skills of artisan gods
and live by deftness of the eye and hand,
and some have won the muses' gifts
and sing in verse the wisdom of the ages.
Yet other men Apollo has made seers
who sight the evil Gods prepare for men.
But what is destined, no omen can repel
or poetry or bravery prevent.

The Ship of State

(from Alcaeus)

I am bewildered by conflicting winds.
One wave hits us to starboard,
another to port, and our dark ship
shivers between them,
fighting through the storm.
The bilge water is washing round the mast,
the sail is beginning to split and slacken,
the rudder is out of control.

A new wave is breaking over us.
It will swamp us again and we must
bail hard and patch the planks
and run for a good harbour.
Keep up your courage. There are bigger
waves ahead. Just remember,
we have been through all this before.
If every man keeps steady
we shall still be safe.

Paraphrases from Taoism

(freely from the Tao Te Ching*)*

The sky has been there for ever
and the earth is ancient.
They survive because they exist
not for themselves. The wise man
effaces himself
and so he is foremost.

*

You build a house with walls
but you live in the space
between the walls, which is empty.
You use a bowl because of
the part that is empty,
but the emptiness
depends on the bowl.
We live by what is
and the void within it.
There is no map to be had
of the Way, there are
no words to describe it.
It exists, and is not.

*

You can know the World
without leaving your house.
You do not need windows
to see the Way.
The farther you journey
the less you learn.
Therefore the wise man
learns without going,
perceives without seeing,
and does without acting.

*

The more regulations there are, the poorer people become.
The more soldiers there are, the more unruly the state.
The more skills there are, the more frivolity flourishes.
The more laws there are, the more criminals emerge.
Therefore the Wise Man says:
If I let well alone, the people will improve.
If I stay quiet, they will become orderly.
If I wait and watch, they will prosper.
If I exact nothing, they will live honestly.

The People Beg for Peace

(freely from The Book of Odes*)*

The people are worn down with misfortune.
They need peace, and heaven only sends
famines and plagues, and everywhere
there is death and disorder.
The voice of the people is dark.
and their grief uncomforted.
The heavens are pitiless!
The strife is unceasing;
everywhere it grows
and the people beg for peace.

The Diamond on the Grass

(from Xavier Forneret)

It is said, I believe, that the glow worm announces by his appearance, more or less luminous, more or less fresh, whether near to a certain spot — for always according to the saying he moves under the influence of what is to come — the glow worm foretells either a storm at sea or a revolution on the earth. At such times he is dull, brightens and goes out. There is to be a miracle; he becomes hardly visible. There is to be a murder; he glows red. There is to be snow; his feet turn black. There is to be cold; he burns with a steady brilliance. There is to be rain; he moves his position. There are to be public festivals; he quivers in the grass and sheds innumerable little jets of light. There is to be hail; he moves jerkily. There is to be wind; he seems to bury himself in the earth. There is a beautiful sky for the morrow; he turns blue. There is a lovely night; he makes stars in the grass almost as if for a public festival, except that he does not flicker. For the birth of a child, the glow worm is white. Finally, at the hour when a strange destiny is fulfilled, the glow worm is yellow.

I do not know how much these sayings should be believed, but here they are and I tell my story.

On an evening when all the breath of angels glided over men's faces; on one of those evenings when one longs for a thousand lungs to give them all to the air that seems to come from the gardens of heaven; under old and gigantic trees planted among the blades of grass, a pavilion spread out toward the moon its oblong and dilapidated wings.

There was water that wept as it flowed over a bed of thorns. There were many green stones in which the fingers of time had made great holes, and there was much moss around these stones. There were many withered leaves from three or four seasons ago. There was much mystery, much silence, and all that had human life seemed far away. Here a man might think himself the first or the last man, at the Creation or at the Last Judgment. To each leaf on the old trees, to each stone of the pavilion, to the water that flowed away and the briars that hindered it, the moon offered her solemn melancholy and her white tears. But soon she grew tired of looking on the earth, drew over herself for a moment a veil that was almost black, and then there was nothing more to illumine the things of that abandoned spot but a soft fire on the grass. It was a little glow worm that flashed stars in every direction; it foretold a good day after the night that was passing.

Honeysuckle grew over the roof of the pavilion and slid across the windows, twisting and falling down with age, and when the moon came out again the pavilion seemed like a white head with long tresses of green hair on its crown that caressed its eyes filled with stone tears.

On the flagstones, powdered with dust and old plaster from the ceiling and walls of the ruined building, were the fresh footprints of a man, and light, delicate marks which showed that the foot of a woman had also graced that deep solitude.

A copper lamp, held by a cord of pink silk, flickered almost imperceptibly in the middle of the ruin. Its wicks, which had obviously been burning through the night, still gave their feeble light. On this lamp was a shade like that of a dark lantern, and on the shade a brown ribbon attached to the only remaining arm of a seat; the other arm had fallen in the battle of years. The seat was large and upholstered in what had once been aramanthine velvet. It was evident that the two persons who used it must have held each other very closely. Many parts of the seat were covered in dust, but others shone — rubbed, polished, almost worn away by the bodies of those who sat there.

The seat faced the lamp, which hung a little way from it and a little way from the ground.

As well as the running of water outside, something could be heard rustling in all the corners of the pavilion, and when the moon glanced into some of these corners, the eye could make out objects like large splashes of jet black ink which chance had given feet to move over a white sheet of paper; things walking, stopping, moving on again, and throwing beneath them tracks of reflections such as flash from the wings of happy cicadas, or from soap bubbles in the

240

sun, or from the scales of fish seen at a certain time of day; a tribe of spiders in whole families, with their gear of webs, the despair of flies and solace of cut fingers. There the spider could display itself in freedom, fearing neither the cries of children and women that betray its presence, nor the servant's stupefying duster, nor the crushing soles of shoes and slippers, not even the tongue of the burning candle. The spider lived there, secure in his dusty domain. For him the glow worm need not project its colour of a strange fate, its ominous yellow. The spider span for itself a silken happiness, in which all days, all hours, each minute and each second, were sweet and unchanging.

On the seat and throughout the pavilion flower petals had fallen, and at the right, in front of the seat, was a little cushioned bench, and under the bench, like a drawer, stood an Ussassi casket that had often been taken out and replaced, so that its corners were blunted and splintered from having been so touched and handled.

At a moment when the moon looked down, when the spider span, when the glow worm glowed, the ninth hour struck.

The water ran on, as time passes always.

And soon, along a path of earth and sand, a young woman appeared. Her white dress blew under the mouth of the wind. Her hair rippled like golden waves on a breast as white as her dress and as breathless as her hair. Her mouth — her mouth — one could say that it pressed on lips, so much did it tremble and throb with that voluptuous agitation which exists only when lips are on lips, when heart is on heart. Her features shone with hope. In the most hidden of her looks was the death that often gives happiness; you know that death which comes in a shiver that takes one, in a pressure that ties the veins, in an ecstasy that halts life and drains the warmth of the blood; you know?

You see, that woman was going to meet her lover. And she believed in God. In God, in the saints, in the angels, in everything. O, yes, she believed. If you could have seen her heart leap in her breast in the midst of her holy beliefs, you would have said to yourself: "What possesses this woman? Ah, what possesses this woman?" And, however strong and well armed you might have been, if she

could have read the thoughts in your face she would have answered:
"Away! Away! Let me pass! I am going to my lover, and even if
on my way I leave on your sword a portion of my body — even some
of my bones, broken, splintered and bruised — so long as I still have
enough to give breath to his kiss, a smile to his mouth, a look to his
eyes, a tear to his soul, then let my blood flow from the point of your
sword, let my flesh open and spread out under its edge — it matters
little to me, it matters little! But in your mercy, my Lord, my Lord,
let me go to meet my lover, let me go to the paradise of Heaven!"

And she went, she went, the young woman, stroking the earth with
her feet, as if she had kissed it, perfuming the flowers and the air
as she went, and leaving everywhere a little of her breath, a little of
her soul.

She said: "I go to look at him, to speak to him, to hear and
touch him. All this I will have. My voice will mingle with his, but
his is a thousand times sweeter. If you only heard it! Truly I shall
die with those words from his heart. You cannot conceive how he
says, 'I love you!' No, for he never says it and I hear it always.
The sun warms the veins of the earth; for him mine burn to ashes.
God above, how can I hope to tell what I endure? To tell how I am
troubled? When he is there I am aware of something completely
transparent, luminous and pleasing, that gladdens, astonishes and
overwhelms. I hear sounds that first bite into the ear, then caress it,
and finally envelop it in music. I hear kisses, the silver sound of lips,
all around me, and then cries that begin, swell out, undulate and
fade away into extinction. Is that really what I experience, what I
hear, what I see? No, it cannot be. Yet sometimes images, like thin
leaves of gold, seem to pass over my head; whirlpools of spirits, with
wings that throw no shadow, skim over my face; infinitely multi-
chromatic ribbons unroll, spread far, ripple and glitter and fall I
know not where; a Genius, known and sent by God alone, permeates
me with an impulse that strikes me, arrests me, chills me, animates
me, melts me. It is as if I received life many times, and many
times death."

The young woman looked at the stones, the bushes, the grass, and whispered to them of the struggle within her.

Soon, having led the young woman there, the path ended at the pavilion. She heard the sound of its water, and felt again something intensely sweet, and smiled to her little glow worm which had just hidden the moon.

She went in.

The little glow worm turned yellow.

Immediately she fell on her knees, crossed herself and remained agape before the seat. Her fingers mingled sweetly with the tufts of violet and jasmine as she pulled the blue and white flowers from their stalks and threw them on the seat as a little priest swings incense at Corpus Christi. She almost ceased to breathe and a veil of tears shrouded her eyes.

This adoration lasted about the time it takes to say five Paternosters and four Ave Marias.

After that the young woman rose from her knees, sat down, but did not light the lamp, for now she seemed sunk into nothingness, like a machine that has almost ceased to move. She was restless, breathless, shivering, as she waited and no one came. Painfully she drew out from its little drawer the Ussassi casket, to kiss it on every side, on every part, on every corner.

We shall not attempt to say what she felt during the hour when she saw no one enter the pavilion; that would be as difficult as it would be to recreate the world. We know only that a dense cloud stifled her, that teeth gnawed her, that cords of fire squeezed her heart, that she struggled, languished, seemed to be dying under something frightful.

And then fear overwhelmed her when she saw, a little above the dark lamp, the eyes that watched her.

For a while, like two moving nails, they kept her fixed to the seat; then a sudden impulse pulled her by the dress and made her start up, scattering the words from her lips: "Oh, if he were dead! Oh, if he were going to die!" And she ran, she ran, and fell on her lover, who had just been murdered.

On the lamp in the pavilion an owl perched gravely, and at the moment when the young woman ran out, looked at itself in the little glow worm.

On the morrow, at the same time, this glow worm, which had turned yellow for the man, turned yellow for the woman. She had poisoned herself where she fell.